Nation-Building in the Shadow of the
Bear: The Dialectics of National Identity
and Foreign Policy in the Kyrgyz Republic
1991 - 2012

European University Studies

Europäische Hochschulschriften

Publications Universitaires Européennes

Series XXXI   **Political Science**
Reihe XXXI   Politikwissenschaft
Série XXXI   Sciences politiques

Volume/Band **626**

Paul Christian Sander

Nation-Building in the Shadow of the Bear: The Dialectics of National Identity and Foreign Policy in the Kyrgyz Republic 1991 - 2012

Bibliographic Information published by the Deutsche Nationalbibliothek
The Deutsche Nationalbibliothek lists this publication in the Deutsche
Nationalbibliografie; detailed bibliographic data is available in the internet
at http://dnb.d-nb.de.

ISSN 0721-3654
ISBN 978-3-631-67517-5 (Print)
E-ISBN 978-3-653-06866-5 (E-PDF)
E-ISBN 978-3-631-70615-2 (EPUB)
E-ISBN 978-3-631-70616-9 (MOBI)
DOI 10.3726/b10665

© Peter Lang GmbH
Internationaler Verlag der Wissenschaften
Frankfurt am Main 2017
All rights reserved.
PL Academic Research is an Imprint of Peter Lang GmbH.
Peter Lang – Frankfurt am Main · Bern · Bruxelles · New York · Oxford · Warszawa · Wien

All parts of this publication are protected by copyright. Any utilisation outside
the strict limits of the copyright law, without the permission of the publisher,
is forbidden and liable to prosecution. This applies in particular to reproductions,
translations, microfilming, and storage and processing in electronic retrieval systems.

This publication has been peer reviewed.

www.peterlang.com

Abstract

What can explain the constant variations between civic and ethnic concepts of national identity in the official rhetoric of the Kyrgyz leadership? Previous studies dedicated to Kyrgyzstan's ambiguous identity rhetoric and policies have emphasized Soviet legacies of ethnic engineering, a complex domestic political context breeding two revolutions (2005, 2010) and brutal ethnic violence (2010), as well as the predominance of sub-national identities in their explanations. This book, on the contrary, will investigate the tensions between Kyrgyzstan's strong dependency on Russia as donor and security provider and domestic policy challenges, which the ruling elite has to manage in its pursuit of a national identity. The main argument, guided by the theory of Aspirational Constructivism, is that Kyrgyz leaders define the national interest and identity, inspired by both common historical memories and current socio-political challenges, in an attempt to integrate Kyrgyzstan's international and domestic realms. A legitimate national identity must represent both the foreign policy interests of the country, as well as the demands of the titular nation and ethnic minorities for appropriate representation. In order to respond to these challenges simultaneously, Kyrgyz leaders have shifted between civic and ethnic conceptions of the national-self to legitimize their policies in front of domestic and international audience. While ethno-centered concepts of national identity have been strategically deployed to appeal to the ethnic-Kyrgyz population and rally it around the state, civic concepts of national identity were used to appease Kyrgyzstan's national minorities and the powerful neighbor Russia.

Foreword

Kyrgyzstan was once something akin to an unknown star in a distant galaxy. For while Central Asia was *terra icognita* for most citizens of European Russia, it barely, if at all, featured on the cognitive world map of most Western Europeans. Today, after 25 years of independence, that same star has come closer to our orbit, and those who visit it are usually fascinated. Some rave about its beautiful landscapes, picturesque yurts, and welcoming inhabitants; others staunchly hold to their hopes for democratic development in the young post-Soviet Republic, despite the problematic occurrences of the recent past. But it is not only mountaineers, nature enthusiasts, politicians, and journalists who are interested in the small Central Asian mountain republic – increasingly scientists and scholars have been turning their attention to Kyrgyzstan. Anthropologists, for example, are drawn to traditions which have been preserved during the Soviet period; the country's eventful political development makes it an exciting area for political scientists to do their research; and comparatively favorable conditions do the rest. In this way, our knowledge of Kyrgyzstan has gradually increased, though there are some aspects of political life that still pose puzzles - puzzles whose resolution is more than simply a scientific exercise. An improved understanding of the background of Kyrgyz politics can be of great practical importance, especially in light of the major significance ascribed to the country as the region's most liberal state by Western policy makers. For with the position of "key partner of the EU in Central Asia" (Peter Burian, EU Special Representative) and "democratic example" (Frank Walter-Steinmeier, German Federal Minister for Foreign Affairs) comes significant financial allocation, which can only have a real impact though effective implementation.

One such puzzle that remains to be solved is the treatment of national identity in contemporary Kyrgyz politics. In Western Europe we are currently experiencing the extent to which issues of belonging can animate the populations of even centuries old states. This is in part due to the massive migration of people from the Middle East and North Africa – and the many challenges this poses to the political leadership. In young states such issues are often much more pressing and lead to emotionally charged and controversial debates. Following independence, this heated topic took a central role on the agenda of all the successor states of the Soviet Union – it had after all survived Socialism and Soviet-patriotism (at least according to contemporary interpretations) and came to the fore as citizen and states sought new points of orientation for their multi-ethnic nations, some of which only came into being during the Soviet period. The latter applies for all Central Asian republics, including the Kyrgyz Republic.

According to the last Soviet census of 1989, some 4.3 million people lived in the small mountain republic, of whom 52.4% were Kyrgyz, 21.5% Russian, 12.9% Uzbek, while the remaining 14% belonged to various other nationalities. In addition to that, the Kyrgyz themselves are historically and culturally divided in their identity between north and south Kyrgyz, and there never was a large, influential independence movement in Kyrgyzstan. An attempt to define the new state as a civic nation that would consist of all those who subscribe to its political creed regardless of their ethnicity and religion therefore suggests itself to the external observer. And it seems that this was the initial intention of first President Askar Akaev, too. Akaev was unexpectedly elected to office in 1990, and throughout his close to 15-year tenure, references to Kyrgyzstan as the "common home" of all its inhabitants were customary. By the mid-1990s, however, Akaev decided that this definition was not sufficient. He introduced a second vision of Kyrgyzstan, based entirely on terms of ethnicity. Rather than shared political rights, it was cultural myth and bloodlines that determined the discourse of "belonging."

Akaev maintained both concepts of Kyrgyzstan for the rest of his rule, and seemed reluctant to allow for one to dominate over the other. His successors picked upon this double-identity narrative and adjusted Akaev's framework according to their own interpretations. Despite the coexistence of these two concepts, the last twenty years have seen the notion of "Kyrgyz" gradually replace the notion of "Kyrgyzstani." This is evinced by numerous examples, such as the increasing number of anniversaries and historical movies which celebrate historic achievements that are often of a factually dubious nature. Such is the life of the warrior Manas, a mythical heroic figure from the 9th century. Manas' life is recounted in an epic of the same name, which after being transmitted orally for centuries, is considered the most important work of Kyrgyz literature and, according to the Kyrgyz interpretation, the longest poem in world literature. During my first visit to Kyrgyzstan in 1995 it was possible to encounter him if one listened and looked closely, whereas today the hero has become so ubiquitous that a visitor would have to be blind and deaf to miss him. Unlike the neighboring Kazakhs, the Kyrgyz did not turn away from their language during the Soviet period, even in the north and in the capital Kyrgyz was spoken in the 1990's, although Russian was used on official occasions. Today Russian retains an important—in the opinion of nationalists too important—position, but even so more Kyrgyz is now spoken in the cities of the north than in the past. After more than twenty years of academic engagement with the country I have been able to observe this gradual advance of the Kyrgyz language visually: In the mid-nineties Akaev campaigned bilingually, with Russian slogans written above their Kyrgyz equivalents. In the course of his first presidential campaign in 2005, Kurmanbek Bakiev also made use of bilingual posters—but this time with the Russian slogans written underneath the Kyrgyz. And during the most recent election of the current president Almasbek Atambaev the campaign Bishkek even made use of placards written solely in Kyrgyz. However, Russians continue to live in Kyrgyzstan, many of whom do not speak Kyrgyz and have no intention of learning the language. Similarly, in many towns in Kyrgyzstan's south Uzbek continues to be the dominant language.

The shifting usage of the different concepts of national identity was of course noted early on by observers of Kyrgyzstan's political life, and a wide array of explanations for this phenomenon have been put forth. All of these have a shared focus on the inner life of the country: domestic conflicts or occurrences, as well as the often cited north-south divide of the Kyrgyz ethnos have been proposed as causes for this tendency to draw upon the "national concept," just as for example remnants of Soviet thought have been used as a basis for the "civic concept." While they are all more or less convincing, several questions remain. The author of this book has undertaken the addition of another important component to these existing models: foreign interests and dependence relationships—i.e. in the case of Kyrgyzstan the Russia factor. Since his engagement with foreign policy has not been conducted solely from the library desk – as is often the case with this research subject—but is founded on several months of field research in Kyrgyzstan, Paul Sander can draw upon a broad base of material. And as a result he is able to convincingly argue that the Russian component, underscored by the fact that Kyrgyzstan is in many ways dependent on the Kremlin's goodwill, has had great influence on the way in which the topic of national identity is officially discussed. It follows that the changing use of the "civic" and "ethnic identity" concepts can be traced to the debate's audience. In a Kyrgyz-language speech at a rally in Naryn or Jalalabad it makes sense to use the "ethnic concept," while on the occasion of a state visit by Russian president Vladimir Putin it is in the state's interests to present Kyrgyzstan as a country in which ethnic Russians are not a minority, but rather full-fledged citizens, who can live and pursue their interests in a country of Kyrgyzstanis. This conclusion is of great importance for further observation and interpretation of the role that Kyrgyz nationalism plays in the development of a concept of identity and helps to explain the discrepancy in the behavior of Kyrgyz politicians between their usage of the "civic concept" and the simultaneous support for all things "Kyrgyz." Additionally, it highlights the wide reaching implications that the close relationship with Russia can have for Central Asian states.

This topic remains relevant as Kyrgyzstan's domestic and foreign trajectories appear less predictable than that of its neighboring states, due to the country's eventful but unstable internal politics, poverty, great dependence on financial support from abroad, and not least its geopolitical position. Heated debates on national identity are not limited to newly independent states, as we can now clearly perceive and observe in the EU. Let us hope that Kyrgyzstan will succeed in charting a path between the inclusive concept of a "common home" and the exclusive "Kyrgyzstan for the Kyrgyz," between independent statehood and dependence on foreign actors, and that the continuously growing knowledge of the country can contribute to Kyrgyzstan receiving the right support.

Beate Eschment, Central Asia Specialist, Editor of Zentralasien-Analysen
www.laender-analysen.de/zentralasien

Acknowledgement

To all the inspiring people I have met throughout my work on this little project; to those who taught, supported, informed, read and questioned; and to those who simply are or became friends and family to me.

Table of Contents

I. Introduction 1
   1. Research Puzzle 1
   2. Hypotheses 3
   3. Methodology and Data 4
   4. Relevance 6
   5. Chapter Outline 6

II. Literature Review – Nation-building in Central Asia 9
   1. The New Central Asia – Building National Identity
      from Scratch 9
   2. Nation-building attempts in Kyrgyzstan 11

III. Theoretical Chapter – The Dialectics of Foreign
     Policy and National Identity 19
   1. The Sociological Turn in International Relations 19
   2. Aspirational Constructivism – Framing Kyrgyzstan's
      Pursuit of a National Identity 20
   3. Extending the Framework: The Concept of Diaspora in
      Constructivist Theory 23
   4. Nationalism, Nation-building and Competing National
      Self-Images in the Kyrgyz Republic 26

IV. Russia in Central Asia: Fixing the Dysfunctional
     Family-Relations? 29
   1. Russian Objectives in Central Asia - An Overview 29
   2. Maintaining Influence: The Russian Tool-Kit in Central Asia 31
   3. Kyrgyzstan – Russia's Outpost in the Heart of Asia 37

V. Askar Akaev (1991–2005) – Building a "Common Home" for Kyrgyzstan's Multi-Ethnic Society? 41
1. First Term: 1991–1995 41
2. Second Term: 1995–2000 51
3. Third Term: 2000–2005 57

VI. The Second President: Kurmanbek Bakiev (2005–2010) 61
1. The Tulip Revolution..61
2. "The Discrepancy between Form and Content" 64
3. Bakiev's Downfall and the Russian Hand in the 2010 Revolution..69
4. Identity Politics from Akaev to Bakiev: Between Persistence and Change...72

VII. The Third President: Roza Otunbaeva (2010–2011).........73
1. Another "Revolution" 73
2. The Dialectics of National Identity and Foreign Policy Reconsidered: The Demise of the "Common Home" 75

Conclusion 85

Bibliography 91

I. Introduction

1. Research Puzzle

In the wake of the Soviet collapse, 15 countries across Eastern Europe and Eurasia have been struggling to define – or redefine – themselves and their place in the world. Unequal at birth, the Soviet successor states have entered the world under very different preconditions and very different ways of conceiving their national identity (Huskey 2006: 111).

For the Central Asian states, independence came suddenly and was not necessarily wanted. There had been no historical memory of a nation lost, nor had there been nationalist movements preparing the ground, unlike in Armenia, Georgia and the Baltic States. The Muslim republics of the USSR had been created by decrees issued between 1924 and 1936. Not only did they determine their frontiers, but also their names, their reinvented pasts, the definition of ethnic groups and even their languages (Roy 2000: vii). In the face of independence, their leaders had to develop a national idea that would solidify the people's recognition of post-Soviet statehood (Marat 2008b: 16), secure their political pre-eminence within the new citizen-polities, and assert their nation's position within a new world order (Bohr 1998: 139).

Perhaps nowhere in the region has this endeavor been more difficult than in the Central Asian country of Kyrgyzstan. There, history and geography have dealt the leaders a particularly difficult hand. The Kyrgyz Republic has an unenviable location and limited natural resources (Huskey 2006: 111). The Kyrgyz titular ethnic group, which itself is divided by region, tribe, and clan, accounted for only a bare majority of the population in the early 1990s (Collins 2006: 98). Moreover, Kyrgyzstan is encircled by powerful neighbors, two of which, Russia and China, are permanent members of the U.N. Security Council. Their conflicting economic and geopolitical interests, combined with the ethnic patchwork of the Central Asian republics, add up to a field of tension, in which the small mountainous republic has to stand its ground. With Uzbekistan, Central Asia's strongest military power, neighborhood relations have been conflict prone from the outset (Fawn 2003: 126–27). Therefore, in defining a national identity for Kyrgyzstan, the challenge for the country's first president, Askar Akaev, was to deliver a national self-image that was acceptable not only to polarized ethnic constituencies at home, but also to key international actors challenging the country's stability (Huskey 2006: 112).

Akaev's definition of citizenship in the early years of independence was the most liberal among the Central Asian states. Right from the outset, he differentiated between the concepts of "nationality" (*natsional'nost'*[1]) and "people" (*narod*). While the first category referred to ethnic groups, the second embodied a more inclusive, civic-based understanding almost synonymous with citizenship (Marat 2008a: 14).

By the end of the 1990s, however, Akaev had abandoned his initial idea of citizenship as a central element of the state ideology and shifted towards a concept of *ethnogenesis* (ibid. 16). Ethnic symbols and rhetoric portraying the country as home primarily to its Kyrgyz population became dominant. Thereafter, Akaev maintained and moved between two contradictory visions of Kyrgyzstan, one ethnic and one civic. Manifestations of Kyrgyzstan's state-sponsored national identity during public speeches, or by means of policies intended to regulate the country's inter-ethnic relations, have remained contradictory, inconsistent and subject to constant redefinitions. This tendency has continuously been reflected in the policies and statements of his successors, namely Kurmanbek Bakiev, Roza Otunbaeva and Almazbek Atambaev (Laruelle 2012: 42), and poses the broader research puzzle that this book seeks to address:

What explains the constant variations between civic and ethnic conceptions of national identity in the official rhetoric of the Kyrgyz leadership between 1991 and 2012?

Previous studies dedicated to Kyrgyzstan's ambiguous identity rhetoric and policies have emphasized Soviet legacies of ethnic engineering, a complex domestic political context culminating in two revolutions (2005, 2010) and brutal ethnic violence (2010), as wells as sub-national identities, such as clan structures, to explain the observed variation. This book, on the contrary,

---

1 The "Modified Library of Congress Transliteration System" is used for Russo-English transliteration, excluding names that have an already established alternative spelling in the English language, see: http://www.mml.cam.ac.uk/slavonic/courses/ugrad/transonline-1.pdf, retrieved 13/02/2016.

intends to investigate the tension between Kyrgyzstan's strong dependency on Russia as security provider (Bernard 2005; Olcott 1996a: 110) and domestic policy challenges (Bogatyrev 2007; Muzakulova & Dyatlenko 2012: 31; Hanks 2011), which the ruling elite has to manage in its pursuit of a national identity concept. Such a concept must represent both the foreign policy interests of the state, as well as the demands of the titular nation and ethnic minorities for appropriate representation. In neighboring multi-ethnic Kazakhstan, similar problems can be observed. There, foreign policy discourse and identity are closely intertwined, too (Cummings 2003: 140). However, in Kazakhstan, the political elite is much less vulnerable than it is in Kyrgyzstan: The pluralistic and self-confident character of the Kyrgyzstani society (Megoran 2001: 125; Bingol 2010: 49; Saivetz & Jones 1994: 91) and the small country's strong economic dependence from international aid funds and Kyrgyz migrant workers (The World Bank 2013) in Russia have exposed the country's elite to strong domestic and international pressure (Engvall 2015:11; Cummings et. al. 2013: 453; Anderson 1999: 98). In addition, permanent political crises prevent the development of a long-term perspective for the country (Hanks 2011: 185–86). Given Kyrgyzstan's unique geopolitical position, this book proposes the following hypotheses:

2. Hypotheses

1. Kyrgyzstan's leadership has to maintain a delicate balance of tensions and dynamics created and conditioned by domestic and foreign policy challenges. It has deployed identity rhetoric strategically to legitimize foreign policy alignments and to appease both international partners and its multi-ethnic population (This has created a foreign policy – national identity nexus).
    1.1. Ethnic concepts of national identity have been deployed to appease the ethnic Kyrgyz population and rally them around the state;
    1.2. Civic concepts of national identity have been used to appease national minorities and international donors.
2. Kyrgyzstan's strong dependency on Russia has had a restraining influence on ethno-nationalist rhetoric and discriminatory nationalist policies;
    2.1. The Russian diaspora has had a weak influence on official identity rhetoric and identity policies within Kyrgyzstan;

2.2. Russia accepts ethno-nationalist state building measures in Kyrgyzstan as trade-off for policy alignment.

3. Methodology and Data

This book is a small-n focused and structured study of the legislative periods of Kyrgyzstan's first three presidents: 1) Askar Akaev (1991–2005), 2) Kurmanbek Bakiev (2005–2010), and the Interim-Government under 3) Roza Otunbaeva (2010–2011). The case studies themselves will focus on moments of political crisis, when Kyrgyzstan's national identity experienced "teachable moments" (Prizel 1998: 2) and the variations in discourse have been the most significant. The periods of 2005/06 and 2010/11, which mark the two revolutions and subsequent ethnic violence in the south of Kyrgyzstan in 2010 during the interim-government of Roza Otunbaeva, deserve particular attention in this context.

The changes in the leadership's identity rhetoric will be detected and evaluated by means of a **critical discourse analysis.** Such an analysis engages in textual analysis of language use in social interaction. With respect to Fairclough (1995: 132), discursive practices – through which texts are produced (created) and consumed (received and interpreted) – are regarded an important form of social practice which both reproduces and changes knowledge, identities and social relations including power relations, and at the same time is also shaped by other social practices and structures. Thus, discourse is in a dialectical relationship with other social dimensions. Discursive practices contribute to the creation and reproduction of unequal power relations between social groups – for example, between social classes, women and men, and of utmost importance for this book, between ethnic minorities and the majority (Jorgensen & Phillips 2002: 61–62).

Assuming that a plurality of causal conditions ($x1+x2+x3...+xn$) is necessary to be jointly sufficient for producing the outcome (**y = variation in identity rhetoric and policies**), a **co-variational approach** will be applied to investigate whether a specific factor x1, in the present case x1 = the "Russian factor," makes a difference in relation to other variables (xn), to be found in Kyrgyzstan's domestic environment or further international actors. Tracing processes of decision making and linking them to the respective state of Kyrgyz-Russian affairs, and assessing Russian influence that is exerted through a variety of tools, this book seeks to identify whether the independent variables acted separately or jointly to encourage a government to apply or avoid ethno-nationalist rhetoric.

The data which the following analysis is based on comes from several sources: secondary literature, primary sources including official statements by the government, speeches, policy and legislative documents, surveys and statistical accounts, reports by different domestic and international non-governmental organizations, party programs, and electoral barometers. Many of these discursive elements reach the public through official press channels of the Kyrgyz government, and are reflected in the country's independent Russian-language press. Some news agencies, among them the *Kyrgyz National News Agency "Kabar,"* provide their information in English, Russian and Kyrgyz. Solely English and Russian language newspapers, most popular of which are *The Times of Central Asia* and *Vechernii Bishkek,* as well as online news-provider like *Akipress* and *Kloop* have easily accessible online archives. The author was granted access to the National Library of Bishkek, which provided hard copies of *Slovo Kyrgyzstana (Issues 1991–2011),* the most-read, state-owned Russian language newspaper, and *Delo N° (Issues 2000–2012),* a Russian language newspaper owned by representatives of the Russian diaspora in Bishkek. Articles from popular Kyrgyz language newspapers, such as *Agym (Kyrgyz pendant to Vechernii Bishkek), Zhany Ordo (affiliated with Ata-Zhurt party, 2006–2014) and Kyrgyz Tuusu (governmental)* can be found translated on *gezitter.org.*

Furthermore, this book relies on 28 semi-structured in-depth interviews conducted in person with party representatives, members of parliament (kg. *Zhogorku Kenesh*), journalists, NGO and political activists, diplomats, government officials, private sector entrepreneurs and academics. Their first hand accounts offered thoughtful reflections of the policy-making processes that these individuals have been engaged in or affected by. Beyond that, the interviewees provided their personal views and definitions of Kyrgyzstan's nation-building process, its complications and whether or how this process is linked to Kyrgyz foreign policy.

4. Relevance

Kyrgyzstan represents per se a unique case in the post-Soviet identity scholarship. Against the background of the current political developments in Ukraine, however, the present study addresses another issue of regional scope. Conflicting concepts of nationhood, ethnicity and minorities have played a critical role in the ideological battles fought alongside military confrontation: Is a suggested Ukrainian nation defined on civic or ethno-religious terms? Can ethnic Russians identify with the idea of a Ukrainian citizenship, and to what extent do they feel affiliated with what some might call a "Russian diaspora," a popular concept in Russia's current foreign policy discourse. These questions become important, when trying to assess Russian influence in the Soviet successor states, and the Federation's potential to mobilize support amongst its neighbors, and will be addressed by the present book in the context of Kyrgyz-Russian relations.

Beyond that, this book challenges the popular notion that states in moments of instability or threat rally their populations around nationalist ideas. In Kyrgyzstan, it will be argued, often the opposite took place. In order to stabilize its multi-ethnic population, and to prevent the threat of external intervention, the emphasis on the country's international character as a "common home" to its multi-national population has been particularly strong after moments of turmoil and political chaos.

5. Chapter Outline

In exploring the tasks set out in the **Introduction, Chapter Two** provides a comprehensive review on what has been written to conceptualize nation-building attempts in Central Asia, and, to address ambiguous identity rhetoric and policy in the Kyrgyz Republic. **Chapter Three** lines out the theoretical framework underlying the ensuing analysis, which is inspired by Anne Clunan's concept of "Aspirational Constructivism." **Chapter Four** illuminates the post-Soviet diplomatic, economic and security relations between Russia and the Kyrgyz Republic while highlighting interdependencies and Russia's tools of political influence in the Kyrgyz Republic, thus justifying the book's strong focus on Russia. **Chapter Five, Six** and **Seven** cover the incumbencies of the country's first three presidents chronologically until 2012, when current president Almazbek Atambaev came to power. In these three chapters, particular emphasis is placed on the interaction and the influence of the independent variables for shaping the way national identity has been defined by the Kyrgyz leadership. The **Conclusion** compares the preliminary conclusions reached in each of the three core chapters with each other and with the literature, testing the initial hypotheses against evidence drawn from the case studies.

II. Literature Review – Nation-building in Central Asia

1. The New Central Asia – Building National Identity from Scratch

There seems to be consensus among the leading writers on nationalism, such as Ernest Gellner (1983), Eric Hobsbawm (1991), Anthony Smith (1996) and Miroslav Hroch (2007), that, while nationalist movements may create states, it is the states themselves, which create nations, as much nationalists everywhere may claim that the reverse is true. Central Asia clearly is one of the most compelling early twentieth-century examples of how political structures were created first, and a national consciousness underpinning these new political entities was developed afterwards (van Schendel & Zürcher 2001: 1).

The Central Asian nations had inherited statehood as a result of the collapse of the Soviet system in late 1991. Their political leaders quickly realized that the new states had to develop a national idea that would solidify the people's recognition of independent post-Soviet statehood and the new political leadership. Such an idea had to reflect upon the complex Soviet past, accommodate the identities of majority and minority ethnic groups, and rationalize the collapse of the Soviet Union (Marat 2008a: 12). The discourse about ideology became the focus of the elites' ideas about the available means for communicating with the population. It serves as mechanism for linking social groups from top to bottom and for mediating relations between society and state (Murzakulova & Schoeberlein: 1235). For this reason, nation making in Central Asia has been a top-down, state-generated project, rather than a "natural" evolution from language or culture (Suny 2000: 166).

Most Central Asian leaders avoided emphasizing religious symbols and rites in their new identity concepts. This was due to their fear of nurturing fundamentalist tendencies and pan-Islamic aspirations. New conceptions of national identity were often inspired by visions of the pre-Soviet period, when no hard national borders and strict cultural boundaries had existed in the region (Marat 2008a: 12). Hence, many social scientists (Benningsen & Broxup 1983; Gross 1992; Carrère d'Encausse 1979) erred in predicting that all Soviet Muslims would gravitate toward an all-Islamic identity, that religious identification would prove stronger than ethnic identification, and that post-Soviet Muslims would gravitate toward closer relations with Turkey, Iran, and the Arab world. On the contrary, there has been a remarkable attraction of post-Soviet peoples to other post-Soviet peoples, even to Russians, rather than to non-Soviet foreign powers, and the fears that anti-Russian pogroms would follow the end of Soviet rule were proven unjustified (Suny 2000: 164–165).

In order to define their new nations' places within the broader web of potential super-national and regional identities, most Central Asian leaders committed themselves to creating ethno-national communities by re-inventing, defining, clarifying and homogenizing the political and cultural boundaries of their states (Billing 1995: 61). But Kyrgyzstan's first president Akaev chose a slightly different path. He introduced two competing ideas of nationhood and citizenship into the public discourse of the early 1990s (Megoran 2002: 124). The first would have been the preservation and development of the imperial Soviet multi-ethnic status quo, which could in time have led to the creation in Kyrgyzstan of a state of citizens, liberal and individualistic, in which ethnic identity was subordinate to an abstract *civic identity*; the second, constituted the "European-style" (Brown 1999: 295) Kyrgyz nation on the basis of ethnic origin (Brown 1999: 295). These two concepts have been exploited by all Kyrgyz leaders, and each of them has interpreted them differently. But no Kyrgyz leader has defined his vision of Kyrgyzstan as such that it could bind all ethnic and social groups to the state and at the same time reflect Kyrgyzstan's complicated international posture. The following paragraphs examine various explanatory models that scholars have developed when talking about the failure of Kyrgyzstan's nation-building process. Taking into account the theoretical underpinnings outlined on the preceding pages, light shall be shed on what has been written to explain the constant variations between civic and ethnic concepts of national identity, that are reflected in the official rhetoric of Kyrgyzstan's leadership. Which domestic or international developments and changes have represented the greatest obstacle to the institutionalization of either concept? And, to what extent has official rhetoric been reflective of the country's political reality? A look at the existing literature shall provide answers.

2. Nation-building attempts in Kyrgyzstan

2.1. Impediments to Civic Variants of National Identity

Throughout the early years of independence, Kyrgyzstan's first president Askar Akaev intended to portray Kyrgyzstan as a state of citizens that did not overly privilege the state's titular owners. His vision was inspired by the Soviet imperial model that, in theory, had placed Soviet citizenship above the various titular ethnic affiliations (Bingol 2010: 49). For this model to have succeeded, two things would have been necessary: The first is the rapid development of a state to whose institutions all citizens, regardless of ethnicity, could have felt equal loyalty. Such a state would have been based on a functioning economy, an efficient bureaucracy, and a system of state symbols and practices powerful enough to fill the void left by the disappearance of Soviet ideology (Wachtel 2013: 973). The second condition would have been the preservation of the demographic balance that had characterized the Kyrgyz Republic in the late Soviet period. However, neither of these conditions was met. The Kyrgyz elites had difficulties to create robust state institutions out of the wreckage of the USSR, and unfavorable demographic dynamics further impaired the development of an efficient economic and political system (ibid. 974): The demographic balance, characteristic of the Soviet era, altered with the gradual disappearance of the country's non-Asian, non-Muslim population. While in 1989 this group made still up to some 36% of the overall population, by 1999, after less than a decade of independence, their share had dropped to less than 15% in 1999 (First Census in the Kyrgyz Republic 1999). Ethnic Kyrgyz, on the contrary, back in the 1980s still at roughly 50%, now made up 65% of the whole, while the Uzbek share of the population remained roughly the same (about 14%). With respect to the second post-Soviet census of 2009, these demographic trends have continued, with the ethnic Kyrgyz population comprising approximately 70% of citizens. The non-Asian, non-Muslim population has dropped to approximately 8.5% – almost all of them concentrated in the capital of Bishkek, which is likely to become "a Russian-speaking island in the midst of a *kyrgyzifying* sea" (Wachtel 2013: 974).

Already in the early 1990s, the brutal social transformations, in particular the rural exodus of the Kyrgyz, made the promotion of the titular nationality a prerequisite of social peace. Since the Kyrgyz have been granted privileged access to the public function and to law-enforcement agencies, patronage networks have grown in scale and become the key driver of the system's functioning (Laruelle 2012: 41). In reference to this observation, Andrew Wachtel (2013: 975) discerned two complementing processes of ethno-national consolidation in contemporary Kyrgyzstan: 1) the national consolidation of the majority population around a robust ethnically based program; and 2) the marginalization of potential indigenous ethnic competitors within the country. This process was taking place at a slower pace in Central Asia's autocratic states, and a quicker pace in "democratic" Kyrgyzstan. "Because they do not need to be elected," Wachtel (2013: 976) argues, "autocratic leaders can choose not to rally the majority population around ideas of the nation." Astrid Tuminez (2000: 12) holds that, on the contrary, the more pluralistic and competent a country's elite, and if it can operate in a context where free speech is protected, which is still more or less the case in Kyrgyzstan, the more likely that they can help hinder the impact of aggressive variants of nationalism. In any case, the example of Kyrgyzstan is not typical for Central Asia. While the Kyrgyz presidents have remained the primary initiators of national identity programs, it is not their exclusive domain, as Murzakulova and Schoeberlein (2009) maintain.

Following the notion of Kyrgyzstan's pluralist society, authors like Erica Marat (2007, 2008), Reuel Hanks (2011) and Annette Bohr (1998) understand the government's use of ethno-nationalist rhetoric and symbols as response to stronger oppositional resistance from the mid-1990s. Nick Megoran (2002: 164) criticizes the civic-ethnic division onto the Akaev-opposition standoff for being too simplistic. Rather, Akaev maintained and moved between two contradictory visions of Kyrgyzstan from the outset, one ethnic and one civic. The movement between these poles was particularly dynamic at times of crisis, such as the Batken invasion when Akaev leaned on ethnic nationalist ideas to encourage the Kyrgyz to support him. Murzakulova and Schoeberlein (2009: 1243) find that these two divergent concepts, one civic ("Kyrgyzstan—our common home") and one ethnic ("Manas"), though intended for different audiences, must be considered as parts of a single strategy: "where one piece does not work, the other is deployed." Kyrgyzstan's external environment, however, receives no attention in their analysis.

2.2. Impediments to Ethno-Nationalist Variants of National Identity

The rise of a powerful nationalist movement, demographic shifts and the failure to establish an economically viable state based on the rule of law have fueled beliefs that Kyrgyzstan will eventually be consolidated on the myth of an ethnic Kyrgyz nation (Wachtel 2013). Yet ethno-nationalist rhetoric has been deployed with utmost carefulness since the early 1990s. Until the present day, ethnic and civic visions of Kyrgyzstan's identity have been continuously challenging each other and the country suffers from an ongoing identity crisis. In the following, it is intended to identify sociopolitical challenges and structural legacies that have constituted an impediment to radical ethno-nationalization of post-Soviet Kyrgyzstan.

When the five independent Central Asian republics appeared first on the map, a fierce debate unfolded within indigenous (titular) elite-circles on how the new nation states' identities were to be defined. In order to obtain a better understanding of social composition and predominant attitudes among the Central Asian elites in the early 1990s, two Kazakhstani scholars (Amrekulov & Masanov 1994: 165–67) developed a typology that divides members of the Kazakh intelligentsia into three primary categories based on their conceptions of the "ethnocratic" state (Bohr 1998: 140). The *first* and most numerous group comprises rural members of the educated classes, born mainly in Kazakh towns and villages with a traditional-patriarchal structure. Educated in Kazakh schools, they tended to perceive Russian culture as alien. Members of this group who had become fully integrated into urban life nevertheless retain their traditional worldview, which sets them in natural opposition to a russified urban culture. The *second group* encompasses all members of the urban Kazakh intelligentsia, who have assimilated both Kazakh and Russian cultures to a nearly equal degree and are therefore characterized by an "ethno-cultural and linguistic dualism." The *third* and the least numerous group includes the urban Kazakhs, who are both linguistically *russified* and estranged from Kazakh culture (ibid.).

According to Annette Bohr (1998), this classification of the indigenous Kazakh intelligentsia, which follows an urban-rural dividing line and emphasizes educational environment, can be successfully extrapolated on to the native intelligentsias of the other Central Asian states. In crafting nationalizing identities and policies, contemporary Central Asian leaders are guided principally by the members of the first group as well as certain members of the third group (depending on the degree to which identity has been influenced by Russian culture and language) in the typology described above. As they carry with them the memory of past injustices, they seek to redress those grievances in the form of new nation-building measures. The primary targets of their nationalizing measures are not only ethnic Russians but also their russified co-ethnics, whom they regard as having betrayed the national cause (Bohr 1998: 140).

Two contradictory factors have marred those leaders' nation-building efforts since independence: a split from the Soviet roots that gave way to the construction of new state identities, and the fear contained in this departure. The leaders of Uzbekistan and Tajikistan, as well as the late leader of Turkmenistan, developed "a particular aversion to Sovietism," unlike their Kyrgyz and Kazakh counterparts, where Lenin monuments have survived amidst indifference and nostalgia (Matveeva 2009: 1104). However, Cummings (2013: 36) observes that the leaders' new symbolic concepts and ideologies remain in competition with the strong opposing forces of Sovietism and, more recently, Islam. Since both Islamic and Soviet or "Putinist" alternatives are culturally resonant, albeit for different groups of society, the Central Asian rulers are vulnerable and challenged, because these alternatives emanate from sources beyond their control (ibid.).

Titular elites in Central Asia have engaged in nation-building not only in response to pressure exerted "from below" by the indigenous intelligentsia, but also as a means of fortifying the integrity of the titular nations themselves, which has been undermined to a certain extent by sub-ethnic ties and loyalties. Since many members of the titular nations regard their region, extended family or neighborhood as their principal attachment, the promulgation of a national-unifying identity becomes all the more urgent (Bohr 1998: 141). Despite Soviet efforts to eliminate their importance in Central Asia, many authors at present consider so called "clans" to have captured or penetrated the state apparatus of the Central Asian countries, in order to exploit resources of the respective countries to accumulate wealth and further power (Domashev 2010; Collins 2004; Omuralieva 2008). According to these authors, clans appear to be dominant social units which have their roots in pre-modernity and pre-nationalism. These units have managed to preserve through social cataclysms and colonization of the past two centuries, have emerged as hidden actors behind the official Soviet façade of *Vsia vlast' – Sovetam* ("All power – to the Soviets")[2], and have ridden to power with declarations of post-communist independence (Domashev 2010: 3).

In particular in Kyrgyzstan, where a more open political system in the 1990s allowed for public political debate (Bingol 2010: 49), one could observe the rampant rise of clan politics within the regime. The democratic ideology propounded by Akaev and the nascent Kyrgyz civil society in the early 1990s had only had a limited effect; democratization began to erode by 1995, a process actively driven by clans that had pervaded the regime and sought to consolidate their own power bases (Roy 2000: 137). Akaev's reaction to challenges from competing clans in defense of his own position, and to criticism from other opposition groups, included not only political means, but also a major shift in Kyrgyzstan's identity discourse. In 1995, the celebration of the Manas Epic's symbolic millennium marked such a shift (Marat 2008a: 16). President Akaev sought to portray himself as the one who, following in the footsteps of the hero Manas, at last united the Kyrgyz clans by overseeing independence and who promotes a Kyrgyz identity wedded to the territorial state (Megoran 2001: 120). Thus, he replaced emphasis on ethnic symbols rather than on the idea of citizenship.

Another variable in the fierce debates on Kyrgyz nationhood and national identity is the supposed divide of the country into north and south. The country's geographical division, according to some scholars (Berdikeeva 2006; Ryabkov 2008), reflects a divide in political values and differences in the perception of Kyrgyzstan's external environment and allies. Some sources have posited that competition between "northern" and "southern" clans could even be traced at least as far back as the period of the Kokand Khanate (1709–1883), centered in the Fergana Valley. The southern clans had ties with the Khanate, and resisted incorporation into the Tsarist Empire (and later the USSR). The northerners are generally sought to

---

2 "A Soviet principle that instead of being ruled by monarchs, presidents, or some other rulers, in the Soviet Union power is executed by the people themselves, who have convened assemblies (*sovety*)" (Domashev 2010: 3).

avoid conflict and to cooperate with advancing Russian forces (Berdikeeva 2006: 6). Nowadays, as Martha Olcott (1996: 403) notes, the disparate levels of economic development between the wealthier northern and the disenfranchised southern regions might still pose an impediment to national cohesion, including the *southerner's* acceptance of state ideology designed in Bishkek.

2.3. The International Dimension of Kyrgyzstan's Identity Formation

> *"Sometimes it seems as if small states are like small boats, pushed out into a turbulent sea, free in one sense to traverse it; but, without oars or provisions, without compass or sails, free also to perish. Or, perhaps, to be rescued and taken on board of a larger vessel."*
> – Shridath Ramphal, Secretary-General of the British Commonwealth[3]

These words might have been designed for states such as Kyrgyzstan. "Measured by any of the traditional standards of power in international affairs, Kyrgyzstan falls at or near the bottom of the league tables in the lands of the former USSR" (Huskey 2006: 111) Its population of 5.4 million (Census 2009) is located in a predominantly mountainous region in the middle of Asia, far removed from the nearest port, on the Indian Ocean. At its inception in December 1991, it had no diaspora, as the Armenians had, to plead its case in Western capitals. It had no strategic nuclear weapons with which to attract the attention of the United States, as Russia, Belarus, Ukraine or Kazakhstan had. It bordered neither Europe – as did the Baltic States – nor "rogue states" such as Iran and Afghanistan – as did Turkmenistan, Tajikistan, and Uzbekistan (Huskey 2006: 111). It had some gold and a surfeit of water – a commodity of enormous importance for downstream countries in Central Asia – but it lacked the massive energy resources that brought foreign companies into states surrounding the Caspian Sea, such as Azerbaijan and Kazakhstan (Hanks 2011: 178). As a result of limited population and resources, it could sustain only a nominal army of some 12,000 troops, a force too small to guard its own borders initially. Thus, troops from the

---

3   Ramphal 1984: 368.

Russian Federation continued to protect Kyrgyzstan's (app. 1100 km) long border with China well into the post-Soviet era (Huskey 2006: 112).

Kyrgyzstan's foreign policy has been governed by two basic considerations. The first is that the country is too small and too poor to become economically viable without considerable outside assistance. The second is that it lies in a nervous and volatile corner of the globe, vulnerable to a number of unpleasant possibilities. Both of these considerations force Kyrgyzstan to play slightly different roles simultaneously in its relations with the outside world, which has sometimes made the country's foreign policy seem ambiguous and contradictory (Olcott 1996a: 112).

Referring to Ilya Prizel's (1998: 16) note that "it is interaction with the outside world, namely the acceptance or rejection of 'the other,' that allows polities to develop a sense of national uniqueness," Huskey (2006: 116) argues that in smaller and more vulnerable countries, "the other" is likely to have an especially profound impact on national self-perception. Hence, to understand the development of a national identity in Kyrgyzstan, it would be essential to examine the country's encounters with diverse, and often competing, diplomatic worlds. Regional powers such as Russia, China and Uzbekistan on the one hand, as well as influential Western Powers, above all the United States, are considered independent variables that shaped Kyrgyzstan's early identity debates. Martha Olcott (1996a: 24) speaks of "ethnic cards," which the leaders of Central Asia's new states tried to put into play in order to attract international investment and support during the early years of independence. Initial reference to Turkish/Persian, Islamic and Asian identity was soon overshadowed by (re-) orientation towards the omnipresent common Russian/Soviet heritage, which was supposedly the ace among all ethnic cards (Gleason 1997: 146). Annette Bohr (1998: 141), Erica Marat (2008: 15) and Gregory Gleason (1997:138) touch upon the leverage of the relationship with the Russian Federation as well as Russian foreign policy initiatives, which can act as important constraints on the nationalizing process of the Central Asian states. The strong dependency on Russia in terms of economic aid and security provision, Olcott (1996a: 122) holds, made President Akaev more compliant toward Yeltsin's demands than most of his fellow Central Asian rulers. In spite of strong domestic opposition, Akaev agreed to re-examine the constitutional provisions regarding dual-citizenship and the status of the Russian language in the late 1990s.

The international field of tensions, in which Kyrgyzstan has been situated since independence, has received few attention from scholars. By focusing mainly on the initial phase of state-building in the early 1990s when assessing the influence of external factors on Kyrgyz identity discourse, these scholars (Anderson, Huskey, Gleason) have neglected their impact on the persistence of shifts and ambiguity in official identity rhetoric and policies. Moreover, the notion of a "New Great Game" (Kleveman 2003; Mullerson 2009; Shamkhal 2012) has biased our perception of the Central Asian state's intra- and foreign relations. While it has not only taught us to analyze the region through the lens of allegedly competing outside powers, it also does not allow to comprehend and frame the inter-state relation between these powers and the Central Asian states (Macedo 2010: 1). The fine mechanisms and dynamics between Kyrgyzstan and influential neighbors like Russia or Uzbekistan remain uncovered. For this reason, the present book argues that it is critically important to investigate the international dimension of these events, and the role the Russian Federation as main donor and security hegemon has played, when attempting to explain the ongoing identity crisis in the Kyrgyz Republic.

III. Theoretical Chapter – The Dialectics of Foreign Policy and National Identity

1. The Sociological Turn in International Relations

The end of the Cold War posed a significant challenge to the dominant rational choice theorists in the scholarship of international relations. This period was marked by the end of the ideological confrontation between communism and capitalism, and the dramatic developments in the international arena that followed such as the conflict in Yugoslavia. These events could not be adequately explained by existing analytical approaches (Katzenstein 1996: 3–17). As such, the failure of mainstream IR theory to provide correct predictions and to explain outcomes caused many scholars and policy makers to re-engage with the national, i.e. with domestic and non-material sources of foreign policy (Bukh 2010: 3). In the words of Lapid and Kratochwil (1996: 4), "the global eruption of separatist nationalism set in motion by the abrupt ending of the Cold War has directly and inescapably forced the IR scholarly community to rethink the theoretical status of culture and identity in world affairs." At the same time, the conceptions of identity and culture have themselves gone through drastic revision (Bukh 2010: 3), and have become "emergent and constructed, contested and polymorphic, interactive and process-like" (Lapid & Kratochwil 1996: 6–8).

As opposed to the rationalist ontology of mainstream IR, constructivism, or what has been labeled as the "sociological turn" (Katzenstein et al. 1898: 675) in the scholarship of international relations, denies the existence of an objective given reality, within which states operate, but perceives this as "socially objectivated knowledge" (Bukh 2010: 3). While neo-realist approaches, for example, rely on a situational stimulus-response model of national interest, with the stimulus arising from the distribution of material power (Mearsheimer 2001), constructivists believe that interests are more ambiguous. Constructivists argue that definitions of the national interest are shaped not only by the material environment, but also by identity, norms, and other social and cultural factors (Clunan 2009: 5). In some accounts, existing social identities generate social structures that govern what choices and actions are appropriate in given circumstances (Wendt 1966).

In others, social norms shape what actions are deemed possible, given the potential consequences of social ostracism or social mobility (Finnemore 1996a; 1996b as in Clunan 2009: 6). Actors hence react to the current distribution of identities, norms, and practices in the international community. Ironically, while these constructivist accounts seek to chart identity change over time, most of them, similar to rationalist approaches, tend to focus on present situations. Other situational constructivist accounts, such as Ted Hopf's (2000), that draw on cognitive psychology argue that identities are social cognitive structures. As a result, they also give a highly structural account of how identity shapes behavior. Such accounts leave no room for agency and identity choice, and contain no account of how particular identities come to dominate at different points in time and how they change (Clunan 2009: 5–6).

2. Aspirational Constructivism – Framing Kyrgyzstan's Pursuit of a National Identity

In the constructivist approach underlying this study, national identity formation is a process shaped by past and present and by human reason. It is not fixed over time (Demo 1992: 305–6), and it can be reduced monocausally neither to historical traditions and culture nor to present conditions. Politicians, intellectuals, and media representatives continuously instantiate and recreate the country's collective ideas, values, and symbols, but to borrow from Marx (1969: 398), they do not always do so in circumstances of their own choosing (Clunan 2009: 28). Members of the political elite repeatedly interpret and reinvent the country's identity in the light of past experience and new events. Hence, identities are subject to modification and alteration as political elites seek to incorporate current events and experiences that may not initially "fit" with an identity and its prescriptions (ibid.).

In the following, the process of identity formation according to this theoretical framework shall be explained in deeper detail: Members of the political elite develop aspirations based on common historical memories and socio-political challenges. Motivated by value rationality and the need for collective self-esteem, they introduce competing *national self-images* into the political discourse. National self-images are sets of ideas about the country's political purpose and international status. They deploy an identity management strategy – choosing from mobility, creativity, and competition – to enhance national self-esteem (Tajfel 1978: 33). Political elites propagate national self-images in an effort to define "the" national identity and interest of their country (Clunan 2009: 10).

Then, they argue publicly about the practicality and historical legitimacy of the purpose and status portrayed in contending national self-images. This selection process consists of "correspondence tests of legitimacy:" a process of history- and efficacy-testing in which political elites set self-images for their correspondence to aspirations and circumstances (ibid. 37). To test a national self-image for historical "correctness," political elites assess it in light of historical aspirations – dominant memories of the high and low points in their country's past (March & Olsen 1998). Political elites also assess whether their national self-images are "realistic," that is, whether they are effective or practical guides for the state, taking into account the country's historical aspirations as well as the prevailing international and domestic conditions that it faces. "Perceptions of external factors, such as the behavior of other states or international crises, and the perceived success or failure of persons and policies associated with particular national self-images affect whether political elites will view a particular national self-image as a practical guide for the state's interests and something that conforms to their historical aspirations" (Clunan 2009: 11).

2.1. National Self-Images and National Identity

National self-images are "candidate-national identities" (ibid. 12) at play in political debate at any given time. They entail prescriptions regarding what the country should be and do, in other words the country's substantive national interests and its interests in behaving in particular ways in its external relations. National self-images differ from national identities in that they are the temporally discrete conceptions of what the collective ought to be and how it ought to behave (Turner 1986 in Demo 1992: 305).

Usually, several self-images are competing simultaneously within the political arena. If one national self-image succeeds in dominating public discourse over time, it becomes institutionalized not only in the form of domestic laws, regulations, and symbolic and governmental structures but also as stable expectations of rights, privileges, jurisdictions, obligations, and norms of behavior in relations with other states and among domestic societal actors. The idea it entails about the state's international status and political purpose become national interests – "values to be upheld, defended and projected" (Clunan 2009: 30).

A national identity has been established when a particular national self-image consistently dominates the political discourse for an extended period of time. This happens once a majority of political elites are persuaded of the correspondence among national self-image, historical aspirations, and reality: that self-image becomes dominant and defines national interests. Even once a national self-image becomes a national identity, it does not become a fixed but rather a moving target (ibid. 45). It is subject to constant change, revision, and updating as a function of variations in situations and situational demands (Burke 2000: 229). It may be most likely to change or collapse during what Sewell (1996, as in Mahoney 2000: 538) calls "initial ruptures," during which unpredictable events, a revolution, for instance, create "a surprising break with routine practice."

2.2. The Relationship between the National Self and Foreign Others

The nature of a country's relationship with foreign countries serves to reinforce or undermine the legitimacy of different national self-images by affecting whether these images are viewed as historically legitimate and effective. Further, "the national mission and international status inherent in national self-images make the current behavior of those states important variables in the selection of one national self-image over another." Political elites continually test the practicality and appropriateness of the identity and interest in the light of external and internal events; this is the mechanism by which stable national identities are altered and modified (Clunan 2009: 44–45).

It is important to note that not all external actors or behaviors have an equal likelihood of influencing internal debates about national self-images. The candidate self-images themselves single out certain countries and policy issues as central, thus focusing attention on specific actors and behaviors (ibid. 43).

But external action does not automatically elicit domestic reaction, as in the realist and structural constructivist explanations of the sources of state's interest and identity. Elites understand external reaction in terms of a state's own past, which determines whether an act is interpreted as hostile or friendly, cooperative or confrontational, and whether the act itself is salient or ignored. Empirical work in social psychology indicates that not all groups connect their self-esteem to outgroups (ibid. 45). Instead, a groups's "significant other" may be itself over time or an ideal image of itself (Stets & Burke 2009: 192).

Moreover, national identities are nurtured and tested not only by passive domestic reflection upon a country's position and external events within its international context. The active response to external events in the form of foreign policy, that is the interaction with countries within and beyond its neighborhood, provides a platform to express and reaffirm self-images and identity, legitimizing the current leadership's conformity in acting in accordance with dominant self-visions towards the domestic auditory. Therefore, foreign policy, with its role as either the protector or the anchor of national identity, can be understood as the political elite's tool for mass mobilization and political cohesion (Prizel 1998: 19).

In order to comprehensively frame the dynamics of identity formation in Central Asia, in particular in Kyrgyzstan, it is necessary to introduce a fourth component into the society – state – international system complex. Illuminating the role of diaspora within the identity formation process will lead us to question the classic state-centered understanding of the boundaries of national consciousness and national identity.

3. Extending the Framework: The Concept of Diaspora in Constructivist Theory

In accordance with Shain and Barth (2003: 452), the term **diaspora** (gr. *dia spora* – splitting the seed) shall describe people with a common origin who reside, more or less on a permanent basis, outside the borders of their ethnic or religious homeland—whether that homeland is real or symbolic, independent or under foreign control. Diaspora members identify themselves, or are identified by others—inside and outside their homeland—as part of the homeland's national community, and as such are often called upon to participate, or become entangled, in homeland-related affairs. Theoretically, diasporas have been posited as challenging traditional state institutions of citizenship and loyalty, and as an important feature of the relationship between domestic and international politics (ibid. 449). Because they reside outside their kin-state but claim a legitimate stake in it, diasporas defy the conventional meaning of the state (Shain 2007: 127). They are therefore defined as the "paradigmatic other of the nation-state," as challengers of its traditional boundaries, as transnational porters of cultures (Shain & Barth 2003: 450), and as manifestations of "de-territorialized communities" (Nagatomo 2011). With their emphasis on people rather than states, diasporas challenge the efficacy of fixed political regimes and elude their regulation through the creation of new solidarities and the provision of alternative sources of affiliation rather than sole membership of a homeland state (Ong 1998: 20). Therefore, they are considered a critical force in the context of national identity formation.

Against this background, Shain and Barth (2003) argue in their article "Diasporas and International Relations Theory," that diasporic activities can be better understood by setting their study in the "theoretical space" shared by constructivist schools. In particular, social constructivist theories "assume, a priori, that identities are potentially part of the constitutive practices of the state, and so, productive of its actions at home and abroad" (Hopf 1998: 193). Khachig Tololyan notes that diasporas "act in consistently organized ways to develop an agenda for self-representation in the political or cultural realm, either in the host-land or across national boundaries" (as in Robbins 1998: 12). Such assertions imply an ideational realm within diasporas that goes beyond economic, legal or even political obligations or contracts with the host-land, pointing instead to shared beliefs, ideas and evaluations within and across national borders. From this viewpoint, "diasporas act as effectively independent actors which actively influence the policies (domestic or foreign) of their homelands" (Ogden 2008: 4).

The diaspora-paradigm "rearticulate[s] the boundaries of regional and national consciousness" (Robbins 1998: 21) by re-conceptualizing the boundaries and limits between self and other, while recognizing the contentious nature of multiple identity gestation and emergence (Ogden 2008: 6). In turn, the subject of diaspora embodies "a shift from a specifically modern articulation of relations of identity and difference in a territorially organized space [...] to some different kind of order; [...] radically immanent, having no outside, no others" (Walker 2002: 343). Following this assumption, the present study understands diaspora as an independent agent, which can be both a political instrument of kin- and host-state to shape identity discourse, while being itself able to introduce visions of self and other into the political arena of the host land. Through various channels of influence provided by kin- and hostland, diasporas can defy territorial boundaries and impact identity debates by supporting predominant national self-images competing within elite discourse, or introducing their own. The following schema shall provide a simplified illustration of the circular nature of discourse formation between the Kyrgyz Republic and the Russian Federation, highlighting the role of the Russian diaspora's news channels activating Russian reaction:

Figure 1.0

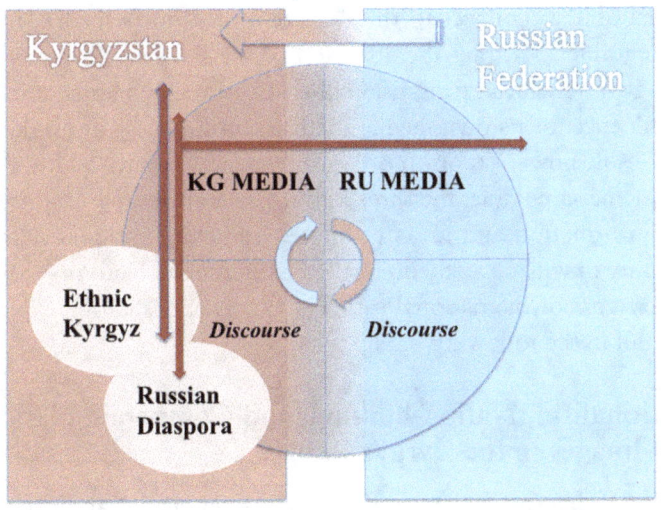

The Russian Federation has several channels through which identity rhetoric and discourse within Kyrgyzstan can be influenced. The *first, direct and primary channel* of political influence on politicians and the Kyrgyzstani government is through hard-power bargaining strategies and is represented in Figure 1.0 by the upper arrow connecting the Russian Federation with

Kyrgyzstan, without necessarily intersecting the circle of discourse and media encompassing the two countries. The *second channel* is Russian media, which produces content that is consumed by Kyrgyzstan's citizens in the form of online and print news outlets, social media platforms, TV channels and radio stations. The media has leverage on both society and inter-state levels, shaping attitudes amongst society and its leaders. For this reason, the *interrelationship* between the public discourse on the *society level* and the *governmental level* on the one hand, and the one between the two states on the other hand, is depicted as circle.

The *Russian diaspora*, the nature of which shall be further discussed in the following chapter (IV), has limited, but not insignificant tools of mobilization and influence at its disposal. Petitions and media channels owned by ethnic Russians can be used to exert pressure on the Kyrgyz government. Moreover, the diaspora's news channels operating from Kyrgyz territory have been able to connect to the Russian Federation's media landscape, thus being able to attract the attention of the Russian government. The Russian government, in turn, uses either its primary channel of direct political influence, or its own media, the Russian Embassy in Bishkek and a range of "soft-power" tools in order to respond to issues addressed in the media. At the same time, the three key actors contributing to this circular flow of information and ideas promote competing national self-images, the plurality of which can theoretically be summarized into *two competing grand-concepts* of the national self. These concepts shall be explained in more detail in the following paragraphs.

4. Nationalism, Nation-building and Competing National Self-Images in the Kyrgyz Republic

When first facing the challenge of building a new national identity "from scratch" (Huskey 2006) in 1991, Kyrgyzstan's leadership introduced two contradictory *national self-images* into the public discourse: One of them defined along the features of a *civic concept of national identity*, one based on *ethno-nationalist ideology*. In the following, the theoretical characteristics of these two in Kyrgyzstan predominant ideological concepts shall be explained while allocating their place within the broader scholarship on national identity and nationalism.

Despite the myriad of definitions of the term "nation," virtually all incorporate two fundamental ideas. First, a nation is considered to be a group of people sharing some set of traits that simultaneously unify and distinguish the group from others. Out of the people's recognition of this commonality and difference arises national identity. Second, nations are in some way political phenomena; "at a minimum nations are the locus of popular sovereignty and the basis for political legitimacy in the modern era, and thus they either have or seek a degree of self-rule" (Shulman 2002: 2). Generally, scholars of nationalism agree (1) that there are many different traits that can provide the foundation for national unity and identity, and (2) that nations differ in the mix of the traits that form the basis of their unity and identity. A simple dichotomous conceptual framework has arisen that distinguishes nations as either "civic," "political" or "territorial," on the one hand, or "ethnic" or "cultural," on the other, depending on the traits that forge their unity and identity (ibid.). There are no universally agreed definitions of civic and ethnic nationhood. Nevertheless, we can identify the features found in many theoretical models (Alter 1994: 9; Smith 1991: 12; Ignatieff 1993: 6–7; Brown 1999).

In civic nationalism, members of the nation are united, or perceive themselves as united, by living on a common territory, by enjoying common state citizenship, by being subject to a common set of political institutions and laws, by their belief in a particular ideology or set of political principles, by their will or consent to be part of the nation, or some combination of these traits. In contrast, definitions of ethnic or cultural nationalism have typically referred to common language, religion, traditions, values, race, ancestry, or some combination of these, which are seen to form the foundation for national unity and the basis for defining membership in the nation. To a substantial degree these two types of nations differ in their level of inclusiveness, "with the criteria for membership in civic nations easier to meet than those for membership in ethnic nations, especially for ethnic or cultural minorities" (Shulman 2010: 3).

Following Rogers Brubaker (1996: Chapter II), the Soviet Union had combined both of these models in a unique way. On the state level, Soviet leaders elaborated the civic idea of a Soviet nation that was supra-national, and proclaimed the fusion of peoples of all ethnic backgrounds. On the scale of union republics, however, the USSR codified and institutionalized nationality through the organization of republics based on single, dominant ethnic groups, with distinct identities, where distinctive national intelligentsias and cadres were cultivated and promoted. "In firmly linking nationality to the notion of ethnic homeland, the practitioners of Soviet ideology generated a belief-system that held that each titular nation is indivisibly connected through its putative history to a particular territory that is the natural patrimony of a nation" (Bohr 1998: 139). This further allowed titular groups to use ethnicity to assert themselves against minorities. Kandiyoti (1996) has succinctly observed that the central paradox of Soviet nationalities policy was that "while officially espousing the goal of merging nationalities and transcending ethnic particularisms, it institutionalized, codified and ossified them" (as in Megoran 2001: 214).

The dual concept of national identity was kept alive in the official rhetoric of the Kyrgyz Republic's government throughout the 1990s, and constitutes the dependent variable of the following analysis. Thereby, the civic and ethnic defined concepts of national identity shall be understood as national-self images, i.e. candidate national identities at play in political debate. Persistent changes in the external and domestic environment, or, in Sewell's (1996) terms, "initial ruptures," will be identified to explain why neither concept has dominated the political discourse for a sufficient period of time, so that it could have be institutionalized as national identity. Since Russia as external actor has had particular influence on Kyrgyzstan's internal debates about national-self images, the following chapter will illuminate the idiosyncrasies of Kyrgyz-Russian relations.

IV. Russia in Central Asia: Fixing the Dysfunctional Family-Relations?

> "What is the need of the future seizure of Asia? What's our business there? This is necessary because Russia is not only in Europe, but also in Asia, because the Russian is not only a European, but also an Asiatic. Not only that: in our coming destiny, perhaps it is precisely Asia that represents our main way out."
> – F. M. Dostoyevsky, 1881[4]

1. Russian Objectives in Central Asia - An Overview

The question of both Russian intent and influence in contemporary Central Asia has been subject to controversial debates among scholars and politicians (Johnson 1998; Nixey 2012; Matveeva 2013; Malashenko 2013). The dominant narrative on Russo-Central Asian relations seems to be one of Russia's decline and growing desperation with Central Asian states successfully emancipating themselves from Russian influence while increasingly relying on more diversified economic and political alliances. Nevertheless, Russia has been anything but a passive observer throughout the past decade: new infrastructure is being built with Russian money, its energy companies are visibly present throughout the region, new branches of universities open in Central Asian capitals and goods from Russia traverse the region en route to Afghanistan (Matveeva 2013: 478). The discourse of Russian decline failed to attach significance to the region's strong economic dependency on Russia through labor migration, the threat of the influx of drugs from the region to Russia, Russian concerns about a potential "security vacuum" in the region, and the possible advance of Sino-Russian partnership in international relations. This cognitive failure, Anna Matveeva (2013: 478) argues, can be attributed to the tendency to analyze Russia's role predominantly from a realist perspective of power maximization and expansionism, the

---

4 As quoted in Hauner 2013: 1.

school with which many of the experts working on Russia–Central Asian relations have identified.

Through a constructivist prism, the entire CIS region can be regarded as the last remaining part of an ecumenical sphere where the Kremlin still enjoys the feeling of being a political leader, albeit ever more rarely and with ever greater reservations. Moscow, according to Malashenko (2013: 1), seriously believes the view that a "suite" of satellites elevates its status as a global political actor in the eyes of both East and West. The following is a brief overview that will illuminate that which has defined and shaped Russian interests in Central Asia since the fall of the Soviet system in 1991.

First, it is security considerations that have dominated the Russian Federation's interest in Central Asia, and which will do so for the foreseeable future (Trenin 2007: 90). Militant Islamists are a major underground opposition force in Uzbekistan. They are also increasingly active in southern Kyrgyzstan, and should the regimes in Tajikistan and Turkmenistan start to unravel, they can be expected to come to force as well. Hence, across the region, Russia has been trying to curtail the spread of militant Islam, and to forge local and international alliances to cope with this challenge (ibid. 90–91). In addition, the Kremlin wants to stem the trafficking of narcotics. Organized crime-networks that operate drug trafficking rings in Russia and other CIS countries are a major threat to their domestic security. They have links to militants, who use the proceeds from the narcotics trade to buy arms, recruit fighters and bribe government officials. Following Trenin (2007: 97), these networks reach out to high officials in Central Asia and Russia itself, thus corrupting and criminalizing the affected states.

The close cooperation with Central Asia's ruling elites has also served another purpose. In 2003/4, Moscow became concerned about the so-called "colored revolutions" in the former Soviet states. The examples of Georgia and Ukraine, it felt, could be contagious. The Kremlin became quickly convinced that the "rose," "orange," and other revolutions were part of a U.S.-inspired plot that aimed to replace Soviet-era elites with pro-Western ones and thus forever limit Russia's influence in its neighborhood (Trenin 2007: 93). "Countering colored revolutions became a centerpiece of the Russian approach to the CIS countries" (ibid.). Popescu (2006: 3) goes even further when arguing that Russia has – as part of a broader strategy to cement its own economic and security interests, which he terms "smart authoritarianism" – attempted to develop an infrastructure of ideas, institutions and NGO networks to gain influence at the level of both government and society in the states of the shared neighborhood.

Further, Russia has been trying to minimize potential losses from the shift of energy resource transit routes away from its own territory. Since the mid-1990s, Russia began to use its might, evident in the continuing control of pipelines, to gain a stake in the various deals for energy exploitation between Western companies and the Central Asian states. At the same time, Russia exerted pressure for economic reintegration amongst the former Soviet republics for it still depended on Kazakh grain and Central Asian cotton, and wanted to maintain an important market for its own products (Anderson 1997: 203).

Last but not least, Russia wants to contain outsiders in the region (above all United States, and to a certain extent China) and to strive for balance between competition and partnership with them, while simultaneously doing what it can to keep them out (Digol 2012: 191–193). The following paragraphs shall elucidate the interdependencies between Russia and Central Asia, and the tool-kit Russia has at its disposal in order to exert pressure or influence on both foreign and domestic policies of Central Asian states.

2. Maintaining Influence: The Russian Tool-Kit in Central Asia

2.1. Bi- and Multilateral Security Co-operation

As elsewhere in the post-Soviet space, Russia has attempted to utilize the security sphere to reinforce and demonstrate Russian dominance of the region. Throughout the 1990s, in terms of size, capability and deployment, the Russian armed forces were unchallenged as the dominant military power in Central Asia (Deyermond 2009: 160). Russian border troops were stationed across the region until the end of the 1990s, Russian peacekeeping troops were stationed in Tajikistan, and Russia signed leasing agreements for military facilities with Kazakhstan, Tajikistan, and Kyrgyzstan. Ever since then, bilateral military cooperation has been an instrument of regional dominance for Russia, with the Central Asian states heavily relying on Russian equipment, repairs, and training (ibid.). Justifying his dependence on the pivotal role of Russia in the security of Central Asia, Kyrgyz President

Askar Akaev argued in 1992 "the Eurasian entity hinged on Russia would collapse if it [Russia] ceased to be a world power, with painful implications for Kyrgyzstan as well. That's why we must make our contributions to Russia's revival" (Akaev 1992b: Interfax, July 15).

Furthermore, Russia's norms, economic, cultural, political, and strategic power are projected in Central Asia through its leadership in regional organizations and security alliances. Russia has been instrumental in building coalitions to advance its interests diplomatically, through both gentle and more targeted persuasion (Jackson 2014: 112), or, in some cases, through coercion (Blank 1995: 4; Maness & Valeriano 2015: Chapter VI). However, multi-lateral initiatives, above all the CSTO, have too often proven to be ineffective. Russian policy in Central Asia therefore is primarily based on bilateral ties. Anna Matveeva (2007: 45) states that the Kremlin's Central Asian policy is more a reselection of "pragmatic opportunism" than "an attempt to revive the shared space." This opinion, following Suny (1999: 189) and Malashenko (2013: 16), is only partially valid, since this "pragmatic opportunism" has been interlaced with ideological considerations.

2.2. Economic Networks

Central Asia is intricately tied to Russia largely due to the still-existing transportation network, which interlinks the region with major Russian cities. Thus, even as some Central Asian states immediately considered taking steps to diversify their economies, Russia's economic involvement in the region, and the shipment of Central Asian products via the "northern corridor" has continued to be accepted as "necessary, easy, and low-cost" (Jackson 2014: 109).

Moreover, Russia became increasingly active in pursuing control over Central Asia's energy resources and transport systems. As a major stakeholder in hydroelectric power, oil and gas in the region, Russia has been eager to assure its position as the main purchase and transit country for the enormous oil and gas resources from the northern Caspian region. Over the last two decades, Gazprom, the world's largest energy company and the main provider of natural gas to Central Asian states, has pursued control of all Russian and Central Asian exports, either directly or through wholly owned subsidiaries, in an attempt to lock these states into long-term relations with

Russia (Baran 2007: 136; Jackson 2010: 108). In addition, most of these states remain indebted to Moscow and have often been forced to trade goods or even cede ownership in various enterprises in order to pay off these depts. Kyrgyzstan, for instance, in 1996 ceded majority Russian ownership in two major tobacco firms and part ownership in a number of other enterprises in exchange for debt reduction (Anderson 1997: 203).

Such developments have simultaneously hampered the establishment of new linkages with the West and thus shielded Central Asia from Western states and institutions that promote political and economic reform (Jackson 2014: 108). The Freedom House 2008 annual survey went so far as to say that Russia's new economic wealth has acted as an "authoritarian propellant" throughout the region, and seems to be part of a global phenomenon of "petro-authoritarianism" (Goehring & Walker 2008). The dramatic drop in oil prices in mid 2008–2009, and the reverse migration from Russia that then ensued, however, somewhat implied a weakening of Russian economic ties with the region (Jackson 2014: 109). Besides, China's successful economic expansion over the past few years, reflected in various long-term agreements on infrastructure projects and the exploitation of natural resources in the region (Forbes 18/12/2014), has challenged Russia's economic dominance in the region considerably.

But Russia's economic influence extends beyond the oil and gas industry (Paramonov & Strokov 2008: 15), encompassing sectors such as mining, construction, the military-industrial complex, telecommunications, transport and agriculture. Significant Russian investments have also been made in the hydroelectric sectors of Kyrgyzstan and Tajikistan (Nixey 2012: 12–13). Central Asian states, meanwhile, have taken advantage of Russia's increasingly consumer-driven economy and look to Russia as a market for their exports (Jackson 2010: 108).

2.3. Personal Relations and Political Parties

Another important factor for Russia and the other former Soviet republics since the beginning of their existence as independent countries has been personal relations among the leaders. As a group, all of the post-Soviet presidents had grown up and been educated in the Soviet Union, had been in informal contact with each other, shared a circle of acquaintances, and used a common political and everyday vocabulary (Gleason 2001: 169). Furthermore, Malashenko (2013: 36) holds, the Russian intelligence services gather information on local political intrigues and pass it on to the leadership or the opposition, but practical action has followed seldom. The only exception is Kyrgyzstan, where it seems to have become "a routine occurrence for the opposition to take power" (ibid. 24).

2.4. Russia's Soft Power

As well as economic links and leverage, soft power and cultural links can be used to unite states and cultivate allies. Russia's culture still resonates to varying degrees in the region. The Russian government, "NGOs," and the media have often promoted the Russian language and a specific narrative of Central Asian history, discredited Western efforts, and provided a source of either support or danger to Central Asia's political elite. Thus, despite real historical animosities and deeply rooted sensitivities about previous Russian/Soviet involvement in the region, many cultural ties with Russia have continued and, in several cases, have even grown over the past decade (Jackson 2010: 106–109). Russian language remains the lingua franca for commerce, employment, and education across the region (Aminov et al. 2010: 1–5). In particular in Kazakhstan and Kyrgyzstan, where a high share of national minorities did not allow for radical language policies, Russian has remained indispensable in education and every-day life (Huskey 2007: 563; von Gumppenberg 2002: 997). While they are increasingly exposed to alternative cultural influences, for example, from the U.S., Iran or Turkey, Central Asian youth today watch Russian TV, which acts as transmitter of Russia ideas and culture (Jackson 2014: 109). The local Russian-language media dominate the market in Kazakhstan and Kyrgyzstan, where in 2007 they accounted for roughly 70 percent of the print runs and broadcast time. Several major Russian news outlets (e.g. *Komersant Daily, Komsomolskaya Pravda*) have local editions in Kazakhstan and Kyrgyzstan. Their reports, in turn, are followed closely by the local governments and publics and can have considerable impact on the way in which public and private opinions are formed in these countries (Trenin 2007: 14). Less Central Asian elite's children now go to the university in Russia compared with Soviet times, but many still do (Jackson 2010: 109).

After Putin's re-election in 2012, the Russian leadership gained articulated interest to develop more alternatives to its conventional hard-power tools. But those so called new Russian "soft power" organizations, most visible among them *Rossotrudnichestvo,* have so far overlooked the chance to collaborate effectively with their minority outposts in Central Asian countries, as will be discussed in deeper detail in the subsequent section. Even the head of Rossotrudnichestvo since 2012, Konstantin Kosachev, conceded in an interview published shortly after his appointment, that, to date, "Russia's ability to wield soft power has not been as effective as that of Russia's competitors" (Komersant 07/04/2012). However, in particular in a small and vulnerable country like Kyrgyzstan, its effects must not be neglected, as the ensuing analysis will show.

2.5. The Diaspora Question

Central Asia is home to several million ethnic Russians. They are a legacy of the imperial drive in the late nineteenth century and subsequent Soviet resettlement policies – the early Bolshevik need to Sovietize the region and to strengthen the industrial-worker component, the massive evacuation during World War II, and Nikita Khrushchev's initiative in 1954 to exploit "virgin lands" in order to expand the area of agricultural cultivation in the USSR (Ziegler 2006: 105).

The migration began to reverse itself already in the 1970s. As the republics of Central Asia gradually established their own ethnic elites, politically loyal to Moscow but increasingly masters at home, many ethnic Russians saw a troublesome future for themselves and especially their children. They started returning to Russia, which promised better opportunities and a more hospitable social environment (Trenin 2007: 110).

By the time the Soviet Union had disintegrated, however, 7.5 million ethnic Russians were still residing in Central Asia – approximately one-third of all Russians lived outside the borders of the Russian Federation when the USSR was dissolved. These ethnic Russians permanently residing abroad are officially considered by Moscow to be "compatriots," - literally, "those who are with the fatherland" - a vaguely defined term (Brubaker 2000: 16; Trenin 2007: 112).

Russians who migrated into Central Asia did not generally assimilate to Central Asian cultures, but over time many developed an attachment to their adopted homeland, while retaining "a sense of colonial superiority vis-à-vis the indigenous peoples" (Ziegler 2006: 107). In the uncertain and unstable milieu of Central Asia following the dissolution of the Soviet Union, the Russo-Slavonic minorities began to feel more and more vulnerable (ibid.).

The Russian government under Boris Yeltsin repeatedly affirmed the protection of compatriots abroad a foreign policy priority. Its actions, however, did not match the rhetoric. Perceptions of discrimination against Russians increased as Central Asian states began to adopt national constitutions and promote indigenous languages and cultures. Virtually abandoned by Moscow, Russian national organizations emerged in the later stages of perestroika, in response to the growing sense of ethno-national identity within the republics (ibid. 108). In Central Asia, the Russian groups included Lad (Kazakhstan), the National Association of Russian Culture (Uzbekistan), Slavonic Diaspora and Slavonic Foundation (Kyrgyzstan), and the Russian Society (Tajikistan) (Kolstø 2000: 225). But this strategy of organizing and demanding group rights as Russians has only partially been effective, because most Central Asian states have been authoritarian and, to varying degrees, have been hostile to civil society (Ziegler 2006: 108; Smith 2010: 501). An exception might again be the Kyrgyz Republic, where such organizations have operated more freely.

However, even in contexts where ethnic Russians face few obstacles to organizing and promoting their interests, "Russian national organizations have been small, weak, and poorly coordinated" (Ziegler 2006: 113). For this reason, one of the central goals of the June 2002 Congress of Russian Compatriots was the consolidation of Russia and the Russian diaspora and the formation of a unified "Russian world" (MID Rossij 28/10/2012). Constant infighting and schisms among and within Russian groups have caused them to lose authority and respect among the diaspora communities (Ziegler 2006: 113). They have not been effectively able to mobilize the local Russians (Smith, G. 1999: 501), nor have they had any significant impact on Russian foreign policy toward the region, as Ziegler (2006: 114) claims. In the comparatively more tolerant regimes of Kazakhstan and

Kyrgyzstan, Russian minority organizations have at least had more space for action directed towards domestic politics (ibid.).

The resources the Kremlin has allocated toward supporting compatriots abroad have been very moderate in content. Though financial support for the Russian diaspora has increased in recent years, it remains modest. The government earmarked 342 million rubles from the federal budget for the Program of Work with Compatriots Abroad in 2007, and these resources were to be spent mostly on legal defense and social security. The Russian Language Program comes with a total cost of 1.58 billion rubles, including 1.3 billion rubles from the federal budget (Zevelev 2008). Compatriot organizations do not receive the money directly; instead, the funds are distributed through the Russian embassies and are reserved for particular projects (Ziegler 2006: 120). The official attitude of the Russian government toward Russians who found themselves living outside the Russian Federation after the disintegration of the Soviet Union shows quite clearly "the victory of pragmatism over the phantoms of imperial heritage" (Zevelev 2008). Yet the political rhetoric concerning this issue often has a neo-imperialist tone. It plays a compensatory role in national consciousness and lays foundations for more resolute actions in the future (ibid.).

3. Kyrgyzstan – Russia's Outpost in the Heart of Asia

Few questions remain: What constitutes Kyrgyzstan's strategic importance for Russia? And, why is Kyrgyzstan so vulnerable to Russian influence, reflected in the above-mentioned instruments having greater effect in the small mountainous republic than anywhere else in the region? First of all, Kyrgyzstan, like its smaller neighbor Tajikistan, is important to Russia as a forward position in the region, historically blocking hostile entry into Central Asia from the outside. Since independence, Kyrgyzstan has become a country in which Russian, Chinese and American strategic interests intersect: Both the United States and Russia maintained military bases there, and China is allegedly interested in having its own base as well (Trenin 2007: 88). All together, Moscow operates four military installations in Kyrgyzstan, including the Kant Air Base near Bishkek where 600 Russian servicemen and a number of warplanes are based, and a naval test site at Lake Issyk Kul in the Tien Shan mountains (Guardian 18/09/14). Moscow has been trying assiduously to reduce America's official and NGO-sponsored influence in Kyrgyzstan, and to counter growing Chinese economic influence (Johnson 2004: 46).

Indeed, the difficult economic situation in Kyrgyzstan, which is due in large part to the country's delicate geographical location, is a major reason for its strong dependence on Moscow. With a per capita GDP of $1,303, Kyrgyzstan was eleventh among the twelve CIS countries in 2013, above only Tajikistan ($1,036) and below Uzbekistan ($1,977) (cf. United Nations Statistics Division). The external debt of Kyrgyzstan totals about $3 billion (Vechernij Bishkek 14/04/2013), and Kyrgyzstan ended 2013 with a budget deficit of about $400 million (Centralasia 28/02/2013). Between 60 and 70 percent of the total economy derives from the shadow economy (Omarov 2011: 214). Unemployment is officially put at 8.4 percent, but according to unofficial data may actually be as high as 20 percent (DPI Bishkek, 18.04.2011). According to UN data, about 1 million people in the country face year-round food shortages. In 2011, the UN World Food Program sent aid to the country totaling $17.5 million (of which Russia provided $2 million) (FerganaNews 31/01/2012).

Russia was Kyrgyzstan's chief source of imports (33.4 percent) and its third-largest export market (18.2 percent) (UN Comtrade: Kyrgyzstan Countryprofile 2012) in 2012. Already in 2010, Russian direct investment in the Kyrgyz economy had come to $95.9 million, and Russia provides Kyrgyzstan with further direct financial and material assistance, too (Malashenko 2013: 136). In January 2012, for example, it delivered military equipment worth $16 million to Kyrgyzstan's border guards (Fergananews 18/01/2012).

The number of Kyrgyz citizens working in Russia is estimated to be between 700,000 and 1 million (though the latter figure seems high), who send home $2 billion every year. If this figure is correct, it exceeds the entire national budget, which is about $1.8 billion. There is Russian participation foreseen in all of the major projects under way in Kyrgyzstan, including construction of the Kambaratin hydroelectric power station, which will be the largest in the country, and the Naryn hydropower cascade (Eurasianet 25.04.2013). The genuine interest that the leaders in Kyrgyzstan have toward developing cooperation with Russia can be seen in Bishkek's willingness to join the Customs Union and its largely positive view of the common economic space and, more recently, even the Eurasian Union being established by Russia, Belarus and Kazakhstan (Chatham House RES 2013: 3). Aside from purely pragmatic motivations for participating, the Kyrgyz political mentality is characterized by an emotional attitude about these organizations. "Many of us had our fathers and grandfathers fight for the Soviet Union, and if only for the sake of their memory we need to create this common economic space," Atambaev said (as quoted in Malashenko 2013: 135). This stance even suggests that Russia hardly needs to exert pressure to ensure Kyrgyzstan's loyalty. At the same time, not every Kyrgyz politician considers the country's participation in Russian projects to be inevitable or without alternative, and by 2012 a vigorous debate unfolded amongst the Kyrgyz political elites (ibid. 136). And, the fact that some senior Kremlin officials regard Kyrgyzstan as essentially belonging to the Russian Federation has created additional problems for relations between the two countries. Still, the Federal Security Service (FSB), Russia's domestic security and intelligence agency, has permission to operate freely and on a permanent basis on the territory of the Kyrgyz Republic (RIA Novosti 27.04.2013). Kyrgyzstani security units have been trained under FSB supervision and rely on Russian expertise (VremiaVostoka 27/06/2013; 24Mir 10/07/2014).

V. Askar Akaev (1991–2005) – Building a "Common Home" for Kyrgyzstan's Multi-Ethnic Society?

1. First Term: 1991–1995

1.2. A Scientist's Vision

As established in Chapter III, the construction of nations and identity in Central Asia has been first and foremost a state-generated project (Suny 2000: 166). Moreover, this book is framed by the theoretical assumption, that human agency and elite perceptions are essential to the construction of national identity. The ruling elite introduces competing national-self images into the political discourse, derived from historical memories and current socio-political challenges (Clunan 2009: 28). These national self-images are sets of ideas about the country's political purpose and international status (Tajfel 1978: 33). This notion invites to take a closer look at the personal background of independent Kyrgyzstan's first and main identity strategist, Askar Akaev, as well as at the socio-political challenges that influenced his early definitions of national identity.

When in October 1991, Akaev became the first president, the people of Kyrgyzstan, unlike their former Soviet neighbors, had voted for a relatively unknown scientist. President Akaev, born in 1944, had previously been the president of the Academy of Science of Soviet Kyrgyzstan and, although he became a member of the Central Committee of Kyrgyzstan's Communist Party in 1981, had never been a typical *apparatchik* (Spector 2004: 5). Akaev hails from a Kyrgyz village in the northern district of Kemin, and he spent about 15 years in young adulthood as a researcher of optics and computer science in Leningrad (1962–1977). In 1977, he returned to his home capital of Frunze (renamed Bishkek in 1991) to pursue an academic career, publishing over 100 articles and training a new generation of Kyrgyz scientists (Eshimkanov et al. 1995: 11) In 1989, he became elected into Gorbachev's newly created Congress of Deputies in Moscow, a position that allowed Akaev to gain insight into the realities of political life in the Soviet capital. There he witnessed critical debates over the future of the

USSR and mingled with reformers such as Aitmatov and Sakharov (Spector 2004: 5). As Eugene Huskey (1993: 31) notes: "If Leningrad introduced Akaev to serious science, Moscow gave him schooling in serious politics."

Akaev's election to the presidency in October 1990 has to be regarded in the context of the progressive collapse of the Soviet Union, and that of the violent riots of June 1990 in Osh and Uzgen, two cities in the south of Kyrgyzstan (Carrère d'Encausse 1993: 101). Sparked by alleged reports that Kyrgyz were trying to build houses on an Uzbek collective farm, the riots for the control of arable land continued until the Soviet army intervened (ITAR-TASS 1990; Laruelle 2012: 39). In Bishkek, the population responded to the events with mass demonstrations against Communist Party rule, including demands for the ouster of the Moscow-appointed Communist Party leader Absamat Masaliev (Olcott 2011). When the Kyrgyz Supreme Soviet convened that same month, deputies aligned in a democratic bloc narrowly defeated Masaliev's bid to become president (McGlinchey 2003: 114). Akaev's supporters urged him to leave his legislative duties in Moscow and quickly return to Kyrgyzstan, where, after repeated voting, he was elected to the newly created post.

The first years of Akaev's rule were marked by his attempts to manage the evolution of political legitimacy during and after the Soviet collapse, but also by the legacy of the Osh riots, which gave a voice to rising Uzbek and Kyrgyz nationalisms (Engvall 2011: 21). These contradictory impulses that have characterized Kyrgyzstan's nation-building process for the past twenty-four years are at best reflected in Akaev's early political writings. In his book *Looking to the Future with Optimism* (2004: 196), he proposes a "Democratic Code of People [sic] of Kyrgyzstan." Its preamble speaks from the voice of "We, the people of the sovereign Kyrgyz Republic, guided by the world experience of democracy, perpetual wisdom of the Kyrgyz people and representatives of other nationalities of Kyrgyzstan." Thus, from the outset, the people of the Kyrgyz Republic are simultaneously presented as a single group and one that is divided between the Kyrgyz and the others. Still, Akaev's declared ultimate goal appears to have been to create a state of citizens that did not overly privilege the state's titular owners on the basis of the Soviet imperial model (Megoran 2002: 123). This becomes clear in the section "We Declare," which among other things asserts: "All citizens [...] of Kyrgyzstan, regardless of ethnic background and religious affiliation, form a single nation and are responsible for the worthy future of the country and each individual" (Akaev 2004: 197).

Akaev thus followed the model then established by Boris Yeltsin in Russia, which placed the emphasis on a Russian citizenship (*rossiiskii*) rather than on Russian ethno-cultural identity (*russkii*) (Laruelle 2012: 40). The Soviet double-identity narrative that had compromised Soviet citizenship and the various titular ethnic identities within the different union republics, was supposed to be kept alive this way (Landau & Kellner-Heinkele 2001: 27). However, to make this narrative work for and within the borders of only one former Soviet republic was a very different project. The following pages will provide an in-depth analysis of the major concepts reflected in the rhetoric of Akaev's administration, and analyze their evolution towards the background of Kyrgyzstan's domestic and foreign policy challenges.

1.3. Consolidating a New Nation – The Idea of a "Common Home"

In the early 1990s, Russians, Jews, Germans, and Ukrainians responded to the Osh violence; to affirmative action policies generally; and to deteriorating economic conditions by abandoning, or threatening to abandon, the country (Ziegler 2006: 106–108). From 1989 through 1992, approximately half of the Germans and 10% of the Russians had left Kyrgyzstan. 157,000 persons left the republic in the decade from 1979 to 1988. By comparison, 161,000 departed from the beginning of 1992 to mid-1993 (The Budget of the Kyrgyz Republic 1992).

For this reason, in his early public speeches, Akaev explicitly elaborated on the importance of revisiting the Soviet understanding of ethnicity. More than his Central Asian counterparts, the former president emphasized democracy as a means by which to eradicate ethno-nationalist views (Huskey 1995: 559). In the words of Akaev (1992: 60):

> "Our most important task, our top priority, is to consolidate civil peace and interethnic concord. Without this we cannot carry out any reform, not economic, spiritual or of any other kind."

Following this notion, Akaev signed a decree in 1992 to set up two German National Cultural Regions within the republic, the residents of which would be permitted dual citizenship (Kyrgyzstani and German), and the population given rights to decide certain socio-economic issues. Though some nationalists opposed this development as an abrogation of sovereignty, proponents pointed out that the national regions remained subordinate to Bishkek politically and that the concession of dual citizenship should be treated as a special case (SK 25/07/1992; Anderson 1999: 44).

Moreover, Akaev expressed his thankfulness to the Russian minority in particular by praising Russia's contribution to Kyrgyzstan's development in the 1920s whenever the issue of ethnicities in Kyrgyzstan was brought up in public discourse, and called on the press to avoid "chauvinistic" expressions (Orlov 2009). He mentioned the importance of Russian influence in economic development as well as the introduction of high standards of education and liberal culture to the local population (Marat 2008a: 15). He argued that a multilingual policy was desirable, and, further asserted that while there would be moves to study and develop Kyrgyz, "Kyrgyzstan would never tear itself off from Russian culture" (SK 20/01/1996). In fact, it would not be possible to abstain from emloying Russian and Russian terminology in technology, economics, and culture (Landau & Kellner-Heinkele 2001: 94). At the same time, Akaev clearly felt it important to appeal to the Kyrgyz nationalism of those who were becoming the elite of the new country, which became apparent in the gradual ethnic-monopolization of power by guaranteeing the Kyrgyz privileged access to public functions and to law-enforcement agencies (Murzakulova & Schoeberlein 2009: 1239).

In July 1993, Akaev suffered a first setback when German Kuznecov, then first Deputy Prime Minister and the most prominent Slav in the government publicly purported his "isolation" within the Kyrgyz administration and announced that he was considering a move to the Russian Federation (Landau & Kellner-Heinkele 2001: 94). Akaev one year later responded by carefully outlining his approach to ethnic minorities in the following manner:

> "... we need an elaborate ideology of international relations. In fact, it should be succinct and clear. I would suggest the following philosophy: Your country – is your home. The same with our Kyrgyzstan – it is our common home. And this home was built by all Kyrgyz, Russians, Uzbeks, Germans, Jews, Uyghurs, Koreans and Karachays. They created it, not doubting that they would live in it as a family, forever united in friendship and harmony..." (*Akaev's speech at Kyrgyzstan's People's Assembly in Bishkek*, January 22, 1994, as quoted in Murzakulova & Dyatlenko 2012: 36).

The slogan "Kyrgyzstan, our common home" (*Kyrgyzstan – nash obshchii dom*) was supposed to become a marker for the country's new identity, and often appeared in combination with the term *mezhdunarodnoe soglasie* (international – in the sense of inter-ethnic – accord) to celebrate the constructive relationship between ethnic groups (Marat 2008b: 31). Akaev's idea thus recalled the Soviet slogan of the "fraternity of peoples" (*druzhba narodov*), which had described the endeavor to forge a new supra-ethnic entity, namely the "Soviet people" (Interview 24, 09/09/2014). This connotation, in turn, explains lack of appeal this idea had to those people who perceived the Soviet Union and its Russian mother-state as occupier and oppressor (Aytiev 14/08/2014) and the early years of independence as a "renaissance of Kyrgyz national self-consciousness" (Asankanov 1997).

In 1994, Akaev created the People's Assembly (*Assambleia Naroda*), which regrouped the 27 cultural centers of the national minorities, and cultivated a positive vision of their role in the building of Soviet and post-Soviet Kyrgyzstan (SK 01/09/2004). The Assembly of the People of Kyrgyzstan was yet another example of how Akaev's ideology aimed to create a connection between images of the Soviet and post-Soviet societies of Kyrgyzstan (Murzakulova & Schoeberlein 2009: 1238).

In practice, however, Akaev's civic-based ideas and institutions were not as successful and persuasive as they were to have been in theory. From the earliest days of his reign, his ideas conflicted with the legislative foundation of the country: Kyrgyzstan's constitution always contained the definition of a "Kyrgyz nationality" and a "Kyrgyz language" in contrast to other languages and ethnic groups (Constitution of the Kyrgyz Republic, 05/05/1993).

Although Akaev pioneered the "modern" (or Soviet) definition of citizenship in Kyrgyzstan and the Central Asian region (Everett-Heath 2003: 106), both Kyrgyz political elites and the public had difficulties in separating the ideas of citizenship, nationality, nation, and ethnicity. Several parliamentarians were highly critical of the concept, arguing that it was a terrible mistake to deny the nation's past in order to build a stable future (Marat 2008a: 15). The concept of the "common home" was negatively perceived amongst many representatives of the titular nation, and in every-day popular use, the term *nash obshchii dom* (our common home) was, after a while, denigrated into *nashe obshchezhitie* (our dormitory), a negatively coined term describing "a place where no one takes responsibility or resides permanently," as a former Press Secretary of the Kyrgyz government observed (Interview 19, 27/08/2014).

Furthermore, despite the declared intention to give a voice to the ethnic communities in the political process, the "People's Assembly" was never able to claim more than symbolic value. Unlike in Kazakhstan, where, the "People's Assembly" may elect six permanent representatives to parliament, Kyrgyzstan's *Assambleia* remains politically isolated (Kazakhbaev 21/08/2014). Instead of promoting minority views and concerns, the annual meetings were used to promote the government's own political agenda, ensuring minority support before elections (Interview 19, 27/08/2014), as the scheduling of the huge plenary sessions (*Kurultai*) invites to suggest. "Since Akaev's time, the Assembly of Peoples of Kyrgyzstan has been a political body where individual representatives showed their support of the current regime," said Anvar Artykov, a former governor of the Osh region, who was dismissed in January 2006. "It is a formal body under the president, which agrees unconditionally with his policy" (as in Amanov 2006). Edil Baisalov, a political key actor during the Tulip Revolution that ousted Akaev in 2005, goes as far as claiming that the People's Assembly was a means to intimidate Kyrgyzstan's minorities, portraying Akaev as their only security provider. "The song he played," Baisalov goes, "is called 'stability'" (Baisalov 21/08/2014). In any event, both the Russians and the Uzbek diaspora had independently founded their own political organizations or formed pressure groups to voice their interest and exert influence on decision makers. Both of these diasporas, moreover, had a powerful kin-state in Kyrgyzstan's neighborhood, which they sought might be able to defend their rights in the case of emergency (Ivanov 12/09/2014).

The same year, in June 1994, Akaev identified the language issue as the main cause of the large non-Muslim, non-Central Asian population's emigration from the state (SK 14/06/1994). A controversial language debate had erupted already in the late 1980s, when the language, culture and history of the titular nations began to enjoy a revival and were more widely discussed in all non-Russian Soviet republics (Landau & Heinkele 2011: 120). In line with Soviet theory on national development, the titular language was considered a keystone in nation-building and important instrument to entrench ethnic identity (Roy 2000: 121). The popular Kyrgyz saying *til tagdyr – el tagdyr* ("the fate of the language is the fate of the nation") underlines this notion (Heuer 2001: 24–5).

The revival of the Kyrgyz language assumed, therefore, a greater legitimacy and, for many, a greater urgency in the wake of the Soviet Union's demise. On the basis of enabling acts adopted by executive and legislative institutions, the Cabinet of Ministers issued a detailed directive entitled "Measures for Guaranteeing the Functioning of the State Language on the Territory of Kyrgyzstan" (Huskey 1995: 558). Akaev and his ministers, however, were aware of the Russian stand on the matter, both in Kyrgyzstan and the Russian Federation (Landau & Kellner-Heinkele 2001: 120). Therefore, the new May 1993 Constitution (Constitution of the Kyrgyz Republic, 05/05/1993) represented an attempt to appease both parties. It contained several articles spelling out citizens' rights to employ the language of their choice at work and in education. It also reaffirmed Kyrgyz as the state language and the functioning of Russian, "the language of inter-ethnic communication," and of all the other languages used by the republic's population. However, reacting to Russian complaints, it was proposed to raise Russian to the position of official language in a project for the change of article 5 on language in the constitution. Proponents of the bill held that Russian was essential to the progress of the state's industry, technology, science and public health (Landau & Kellner-Heinkele 2001: 120).

A further step to accommodate Russian complaints while maintaining the necessary level of proficiency amongst the non-Russian population, was the establishment of a range of educational institutions, in which Russian was the only language of instruction. Among them were the Bishkek Medical School and the International School of Management and Business (Landau & Kellner-Heinkele 2011: 145–46). Founded in 1992 through the patronage of President Akaev, the School of Management and Business was designed to train a new generation of political and business leaders in Kyrgyzstan. In September 1993, the political leadership of Kyrgyzstan authorized the opening of a new Kyrgyz-Russian Slavonic University (KRSU), a Russian-language institution that sought to attract students of European and Asian background from Central Asia and beyond (Huskey 1995: 563). The Slavonic Foundation (*Slavianskii Fond*) had been largely responsible for initiating the establishment of the university (Huskey 1995: 145–46). This Russo-Slavonic organization had been established in 1990 as a literary-cultural one, but soon became politicized. The Foundation not only collected books from emigrating Russians to increase the Slavonic collection at the city library in Bishkek, but also, from 1994 onward, organized lectures, exhibitions, theatrical shows, and competitions; it also served as political pressure group (Interview 12, 15/08/2014). Several tiny Russian organizations were set up subsequently, but they had little influence on public affairs (Respublica 18/02/1997 as in Kustov 1997).

In response to the establishment of KRSU, Kyrgyz nationalist organizations, including *Asaba* (Banner), vigorously protested the establishment of the new Russian-language university, which was funded in part by the Russian Government, and which Kyrgyz nationalists called a continuation of 70 years of Russian "bloodsucking" (VB 06/10/1992). In order to prevent such protests from gaining momentum, 50% of seats in the KRSE were officially to be reserved for Kyrgyz students (RP 06/03/1993 as in Huskey 1995: 563). At the opening ceremonies on September 9, 1993, the president stood side by side with the Russian Foreign Minister, Andrei Kozyrev, who in his speech for the occasion compared the local attacks on the Russian language to the persecution of Slavonic languages in Europe in the Middle-Ages (ITAR-TASS 09/09/1993). The same year, Russia donated 74,000 school books to Kyrgyzstan (Rudov 2001: 112).

Among those who have watched the KRSU's efforts with increasing suspicion is Ravshan Zheenbekov, currently a non-affiliated member of the Kyrgyz Parliament, who portrays the Slavonic University as a key instrument to advocate Russian political thought, and as part of its broader endeavor to undermine a self-determined Kyrgyz foreign policy. The precondition to such a foreign policy was always an independent and clearly defined national identity, he argues, which would indicate every sovereign state's national interest (Zheenbekov 18/08/2014). Georgii Rudov, first Russian ambassador to the Kyrgyz Republic, elaborates in his book on the Russian-Kyrgyz relations of the 1990s (Rudov 2001: 338) on Russia's interests in Kyrgyzstan. Against the background of country's multi-national society, education is not only a driver of cultural development, but the key to maintaining long-term societal stability and national security. Hence, he concludes, fruitful cooperation in this field is of critical importance.

Besides the classroom, the KRSU had and still has several further channels to convey Russian views and impact public discourse effectively, such as academic conferences, the deployment of political advisors, and the Russian speaking press. It has considerably contributed to shaping the discourse of "underdevelopment of the Kyrgyz language," categorically discrediting any attempt to upgrade and improve it. In addition, in the early and mid-2000s, the KRSU hosted training courses for Kyrgyz government officials, a former advisor to the Head of Presidential Administration revealed during an interview (Interview 13, 15/08/2014). Dina Maslova, the current editor-in-chief of the web version of *Vechernii Bishkek*, one of Kyrgyzstan's most read and followed news outlets, confirmed that it is mostly ethnic Russians working and teaching at the KRSU. The textbooks they use are produced in Russia, and naturally promote a Russian view of the world. However, ideas conveyed in class would "entirely depend on a teacher's individual political attitude and preferences." Maslova, herself an alumni of this university, moreover criticized the poor state of the facilities, and the lack of (Russian) funding with which the KRSU had to cope (Maslova 03/09/2009).

1.4. The Switzerland of Central Asia: The "Common Home" on International Stage

Apart from developing national ideological projects geared towards the local public, Akaev managed to cultivate a peculiar international image for Kyrgyzstan (Marat 2008b: 44). Kyrgyzstan's foreign policy is governed by two basic considerations: The first is that the country is too small and too poor to become economically viable without considerable outside assistance. The second is that it lies in a nervous and volatile corner of the globe, vulnerable to a number of unpleasant possibilities (Olcott 1996a: 87).

During the first few years of his presidency, Akaev promulgated the notion of Kyrgyzstan being a "Switzerland of Central Asia" and an "Island of Democracy" in the Central Asian region. "We are for a neutral Kyrgyzstan and do not intend to enter into any military blocks [...] we do not want an army," Akaev boldly stated (Bugubaev 2013).

These images played an important role in Kyrgyzstan's appeal for the allocation of international investment and credit in its private and public sectors. Moreover, such positive external images also boosted the local public's confidence in the regime (Marat 2008a: 14). Ever since independence, foreign policy has played a key role to attain domestic legitimacy. Akaev and his elites tested the practicality and appropriateness of their national-self images (and, therefore, interest) in the light of external events (Clunan 2009: 44–45). This becomes even more evident when analyzing the state's media organs, where foreign policy usually occupies page one or two of governmental newspapers, and dominates also official TV channels and web pages. Especially official visits are considered the highest expression of friendly bilateral relations with partner states, which is characterized by a strong emphasis on official public ceremonies and their coverage by the media (Rudov 2001: 133). Again, the president played a key role in this regard, not only as head of state, but also as the primary foreign policy maker in Kyrgyzstan (Sari 2012: 135).

While forging ties with Western countries and international financial institutions, in its first years of independence, Kyrgyzstan had to lean heavily on Russia in economic and military as well as cultural affairs. In fact, Yeltsin's first foreign visit as president was to Kyrgyzstan, and the two countries signed a treaty of friendship and cooperation in 1991 (Rudov 2001: 12). Akaev, moreover, seemed willing to grant Russia large economic and military concessions in return for promises of cheap fuel and industrial investment designed to create employment (Olcott 1995: 362). He even offered majority ownership of the republic's twenty-nine largest industrial plants to Russia, in exchange for capital to keep them running (Olcott 1996: 100).

Beyond that, relations with Russia remained of utmost importance not only due to Kyrgyzstan's economic dependence on Russia and the Russian population living in Kyrgyzstan, but also because of Russia's sensitivity over Kyrgyzstan's ties to the West, and, in particular, to the WTO and NATO. In interviews with the Russian media, Akaev repeatedly reassured the Russian population: "I would like to firmly stress that no matter what new ties we establish in the West and East, no matter how great our urge to integrate into the eastern, western, or worldwide economic community, our [...] friendship with Russia [...] will always be given priority" (Akaev 1992b).

And statements of such kind have not only been produced for external consumption. The interaction with other countries provides a platform to express and reaffirm self-images and identity, legitimizing the current leadership's conformity in acting in accordance with dominant self-visions towards the domestic auditory. Therefore, a look at the self-conception of Kyrgyzstan's Ministry of Foreign Affairs (MFA) reveals a link to Akaev's double-identity narrative. Unlike many institutions in independent Kyrgyzstan that stress their novelty and innovation, the MFA and its personnel prefer to invoke the past (Wood 2006: 13). Thus, the Kyrgyz government could justify the continuing strong dependence on Russia, while simultaneously compromising it with the idea of an allegedly neutral and independent "Switzerland of Central Asia." In an official history the Kyrgyz MFA emphasized its pedigree as part of the old Soviet Foreign Ministry going back to the 1920s and 1930s (MFA of the Kyrgyz Republic, Official Web Presence 04/03/2015). Thus, the MFA can simultaneously be the incarnation of two millennia of statehood and also partake of the prestigious Soviet heritage. "The Kyrgyz stake their claim to a share of this heritage as much as that of the Russian Federation, and thus draw upon a rich vein of legitimacy, a commodity in short supply in post-Soviet Central Asia" (Wood 2006: 14). Most other Soviet successors, by contrast, have been keen to distance themselves from the past (ibid.).

Akaev's synthesis of past and present, inherent in the visions of identity he presented to his domestic audience, was also to be demonstrated on the international stage: The intermittent Kyrgyz independence of great antiquity was finally submerged in the nineteenth century following annexation by Russia. However the 1917 and 1918 Soviet grants of autonomy to sovereign peoples, beginning with Ukraine and Finland, laid the basis for the subsequent *restoration* of Kyrgyz sovereignty in the 1920s and 1930s (History of the Kyrgyz MFA, Official Web Presence 04/03/2015). Instead of being an artificial institution for an invented nation, the Foreign Ministry portrays itself as part of a statehood renaissance enabled by the Soviets (Wood 2006: 14).

2. Second Term: 1995–2000

2.1. Common Home or Land of "Manas?" – Introducing the Official Dichotomy

Already by the year 1994, a change in Akaev's initial leadership tactics had become visible. Even though he entered the presidency in many ways as an "outsider," intent on implementing comprehensive economic and political reforms, he quickly shifted to becoming an "insider," entangled in an elite struggle for political survival in the midst of a collapsing economy (Spector 2004: 21). Former Communists were unwilling to face reelection in a newly created bicameral legislature, while reformers who initially sided with Akaev were increasingly concerned about the state of the economy (Collins 1999: 181). Driven by the fear of being accused of malfeasance and corruption by these groups, Akaev decided to strike preemptively at his political opponents to regain central authority. He engineered a quiet "revolution" by disbanding parliament and installing loyal supporters from his region in legislative positions (Gleason 1997: 99). While the new parliamentary elections were finally held in February 1995 and judged to be "fair and free" by the international community, it was clear that serious corruption and manipulation had plagued the process (Collins 1999: 374; Spector 2004: 19).

In order to consolidate his voters prior to the elections of 1995, and to accommodate the rising opposition and ethno-nationalist feelings, Akaev shifted the focus of his ideology from the "common home" to the Manas epic, allegedly the world's longest oral narration. The epic warrior hero named Manas is said to have united the disparate Kyrgyz tribes in the 9th century and created a Kyrgyz state that conquered territory from China to Afghanistan, from Siberia to the Caucasus (Asankanov 01/08/2014). Akaev emphasized the importance of Manas in his public openings and speeches, and authored a book dedicated to the epic (Akaev 2004). A special governmental committee on cultural and educational affairs extracted seven maxims mentioned in the epic and embedded them within the official state ideology (Marat 2006: 15).

For the Kyrgyz government, the Manas epic represented a congenial option for a national ideological framework: The epic captures imagined and real history of major inter-tribal and inter-ethnic battles and victories, delineates the different foes and friends of the Kyrgyz people and reflects the philosophy of national unity (ibid. 35). The seven maxims captured in the epic were not only the manifestation of another national self-image that would appeal to the ethnic Kyrgyz population (Interview 24, 09/09/2014), but also called for generalized principles of ethnic tolerance and respect for elders, as well as other positive social obligations and principles (Asankanov 01/08/2014). Thus, the maxims represented a comprehensive system of values and beliefs. Widely publicized, they included the following (as in SK 10/06/2005):

- Unity and solidarity of the nation;
- International harmony, friendship and cooperation;
- National dignity and patriotism;
- Prosperity and welfare through painstaking and sedulous labor;
- Humanism, generosity, tolerance;
- Harmony with nature;
- Strengthening and protection of Kyrgyz statehood.

The Manas ideals could aspire for a central role in Kyrgyzstan's national consciousness because of the epic's cultural richness and its grandeur which allegedly had reached a global scale, as ardent patriots tend to claim (Suranova 13/08/2014; Aytiev 14/08/2014). The notion that it contains a "universal" rather than "nationalist" message is again built on a combination of Soviet internationalist ideology and the interpretations of Akaev. What the Manas cult actually implies about the symbolic owners of the country, however, can in fact be considered problematic. Even though some politicians still continue to insist that Manas is simultaneously national and international, popular opinion recognizes that Manas is first and foremost a Kyrgyz symbol (Wachtel, A. 12/08/2013; Kazakhbaev 21/08/2014). First of all, the epic itself is in the Kyrgyz language, which inevitably gives the work a national inflection, given that language is the primary source of national identity in the region. Second, it is true that various other peoples are described as Manas's allies (Chorotegin 08/09/2014) and given the complicated web of Central Asia's borders, the nomadic tradition of many of its peoples, and the shifting tribal affiliations and alliances that have marked the region for more than a millennium (Wachtel 2013: 977). However, Manas is primarily understood by the Kyrgyz as the figure who unified the 40 Kyrgyz tribes and created a state of and for the Kyrgyz. Certainly, others were allowed to live there, but they were subordinate to the Kyrgyz leadership (Wachtel, A. 12/08/2013). By placing so much emphasis on the Kyrgyz ethnos, Akaev challenged his own earlier idea of citizenship as a central element of the state ideology.

The origin of Akaev's Manas ideology, however, seemed rather determined on the basis of political reasoning than by reliable historical accounts. The celebration of the 1000th anniversary of Manas in 1995 coincided with the first presidential elections in independent Kyrgyzstan.

Although the epic's hero is semi-mythic, the government engaged the services of artists and architects to produce and distribute images and monuments related to the narrative (Marat 2006: 36). In this way, Akaev mobilized political elites, scholars, artists, actors, and even the sporting community for the preparations. The involvement of virtually the entire public sector in staging the celebrations minimized the possibility of administrative support for other presidential candidates. While using the celebration of Manas to prevail over his political allies and rivals (ibid. 37), he further alienated the national minorities. Many of their representatives perceived the new ideology as an ethnically discriminating story, which was not relevant to the present day (Interview 26, 11/09/2014). It raised discontent among Russians and lowered their trust in the state. The civic-based policy "Kyrgyzstan is our common home" competed with Manas as a national self-image and enjoyed greater popularity in these sectors of the population (Marat 2006: 39). Soon, Akaev endeavored to mitigate the minority claims by making further concessions on both the ideational level and the policy level.

On April 24, 1997, Akaev issued a decree to prepare the commemoration of the 200-year anniversary of the Russian poet Alexander Pushkin's birth (VB 22/04/1997), demonstrating empathy towards Russian sentiments. Two years later, Akaev inaugurated a monument of a Pushkin monument near the Kyrgyz-Russian Slavonic University in Bishkek with a speech that highlighted the close relation of the Kyrgyz people to the Russian language (VB 08/06/1999). The president remarked that "… the Russian language was and will always be an official language in our country, a language of inter-ethnic communication, and a language for the development of science, education, and culture…" (VB 10/09/1999).

After years of dispute, the legislative assembly eventually passed "The Law on the Official Language of the Kyrgyz Republic" on May 25, 2000, according to which Russian was granted the status of the *official language* of Kyrgyzstan. It should be used at all levels of the administration, the legislature, the judiciary and other spheres of public life (Law of on the official language of the Kyrgyz Republic, 25/05/2000). However, the underlying motivations to make these concessions had an international dimension, too.

2.2. A New "Diplomacy of the Silk Route?"

The Russian financial crisis ushered in a new phase of Kyrgyz foreign policy from 1998 to 2004: Until 1998 it seemed that massive injections of foreign aid, combined with comprehensive investment from and trade with Russia, compensated for the collapse of the Soviet intra-republican system and the failure to find alternative substitutes. In Kyrgyzstan, the Russian financial collapse caused unemployment and high inflation, and forced many people to question the strong dependence on Russia (Pastor & Damjanovic 2001: 10–12). At around the same time, increased tension with the United States concerning Kyrgyzstan's supposed backsliding on democratization and elections after 1998 pushed Kyrgyzstan closer to China. Against this background, Bishkek's trilateral initiatives to great powers started to cement into a policy (Wood 2006; Kulmatova 2004).

Since the image of Kyrgyzstan as a "Switzerland of Central Asia" had rather been an advertisement-slogan that soon lost attractiveness to the foreign auditory, Akaev was struggling to construct a national identity that would satisfy diverse constituencies inside and outside the country. Still, similar to neighboring Kazakhstan's leader Nursultan Nazarbaev, Akaev has sought to portray Kyrgyzstan as "a connecting bridge between the countries and civilizations" of Europe, the Middle East and the Far East. In a formal foreign policy doctrine issued in 1998, bearing the title "The Diplomacy of the Silk Road," the president of Kyrgyzstan evoked the historical position of the Kyrgyz as a tolerant people who have been open to, and enriched by, the influences of surrounding civilizations (Akaev 1999 as in Fawn 2003: 130). It was been translated in several languages, including English, and was made widely accessible on several Kyrgyz government and related web sites as the official foreign policy doctrine of the country (Wood 2006: 26).

In order not to alienate Russia, which was still perceived as a critical security provider, the official rhetoric continued to stress the strong bonds connecting Russia and Kyrgyzstan. The doctrine recognized that the "single whole" that used to characterize the "common historical, political, economic...links" with neighboring countries now had to be replaced by a fresh network of bilateral and multilateral relations. This engendered the document's firm ongoing commitment to the CIS and pursuit of regional integration (ibid. 27). On the eve of his visit to Moscow in January 1999, the Kyrgyzstani prime minister, Jumabek Ibraimov, declared that Russia was, is now, and will remain "our main strategic partner. [...] We are bound by close co-operation within the framework of the Customs Union, by transport links and financial obligations" (SK 25/02/1999).

In 1999, one year after the Silk Road Doctrine had been published, perhaps the most significant external event for Kyrgyzstan's identity debates of the 1990s arose. Seeking to overthrow regional governments and establish an Islamic caliphate in Central Asia, the Islamic Movement of Uzbekistan (IMU) twice succeeded in infiltrating Kyrgyz territory and causing instability by taking hostages and invading villages. These events highlighted the dismal state of the Kyrgyz security forces and caused heated diplomatic tensions between Kyrgyzstan and Uzbekistan (Tromble 2014: 533). The opposition press wove around the "border question" a highly charged ethnic nationalism, since the Batken crisis represented an extreme embarrassment to the government, exposing the absolute failure of the intelligence services, the deplorable state of the armed forces, and the inefficient border control regime (Megoran 2002: 139).

In response, the government increasingly turned to the ethnic nationalism embodied by the Manas epic in calling people to rally around and fight. In calling on the nation, it was calling on the Kyrgyz nation. Thus, Akaev's government again switched emphasis from discourses of civic nationalism to an ethnic nationalism drawing on traditional notions of nomadic Kyrgyz identity and the cult of Manas. The newspaper *Kyrgyz Tuusu* went as far as to position the president as the legitimate successor of Manas (KT 08/05/2000 as in Megoran 2002: 152):

> "In looking at the border and state security, it cannot be denied that the policies and effort of president Askar Akaev in the last ten years have steadily strengthened our independence and allowed us to establish ourselves [in the family of nations]."

The Batken crisis fueled a core fear deeply entrenched in Kyrgyzstan's public memory, the feeling of imperiled sovereignty. This feeling is nurtured by the threat weighing on territorial unity, regularly raised in the context of pressures and interference from neighboring Uzbekistan. Although Tashkent is not interested in the Uzbek minorities across its borders, and refuses to engage in the logics of the kin state protecting its co-ethnics abroad

(Fumagalli 2007a: 114–115), the power differential with Kyrgyzstan heightened the feeling of no longer being in control of its territory. Half of the Uzbek-Kyrgyz border is still waiting to be delimited by a bilateral territorial treaty, and the Uzbek intelligence services were known to be carrying out punitive acts against political opponents (or those declared as such) on Kyrgyz territory (Laruelle 2012: 44), as evidenced with the killing of activist Alisher Saipov (Fergananews.ru 10.12.2007). Therefore, it is not surprising that Uzbekistan has served as a central "other" in Kyrgyzstan's public identity discourse. Unlike Kyrgyzstan's relationship with Russia, the troublesome relationship with Uzbekistan has elicited waves of ethno-nationalist agitation under the leadership of Akaev's opposition, that Akaev eventually countered with similar ethno-nationalist rhetoric to address the fears expressed by the titular nation. The Russian Federation could be considered as an "antipode" in this context, since any reference to or inter-action with Russia has been accompanied by internationalist discourse and the promotion of civic self-images of Kyrgyzstan, which even invites to regard Russia as Kyrgyzstan's "positive other."

3. Third Term: 2000–2005

3.1. The Aftermath of the Batken Crisis: Reinforced Authoritarianism

During the presidential elections of 2000, Akaev sponsored a new form of coercion. The criminal prosecution arrested three of the most prominent candidates for the presidency, and used a language law requiring the president to speak Kyrgyz to disqualify eight challengers. Akaev also offered ambassadorial and executive posts to potential opponents and overtly manipulated all forms of the media and newspapers, radio, and television broadcasts (Akcali & Engin-Demir 2013: 47). On election day, voting irregularities, ballot stuffing, bribing and intimidation were all cited by organizations such as the National Democratic Institute (NDI Statement, 31/10/2000) and the OSCE (OSCE Final Report 16/01/2001) both of which deemed the elections not fair, free and accountable. Tensions between the north and the south, which Akaev had earlier tried to mitigate, began to flare up again as a result of Akaev's policies (Spector 2004: 21), and again, Akaev tried to appease them with reinforced emphasis on the titular ethnos and its language.

In 2001, the parliament rejected the draft law on a compulsory Kyrgyz proficiency test for all state employees (Zentralasien-Analysen 2009: 18). Opponents of the draft law maintained that it would discriminate against Russian speakers and other ethnic minorities. Some of these opponents defended the need for the Russian language and consequently expounded the advantages of bilingualism for Kyrgyzstan. This latter stance was more in line with the personal views of Akaev, as Landau and Kellner-Heinkele (2011: 122–123) claim.

Only three years later, on February 12, 2004, a "New Law on Language" (DN 10/03/2004) revived complaints that Russian, the official language, supposedly equal in status to Kyrgyz, was in fact equal "merely on paper" (Amelina 2004). Though it acknowledged Russian as an official language and it's use in certain regions and for documents if needed, official correspondence, in particular amongst government officials and the military, was supposed to be held in Kyrgyz.

To appease Russian concerns, Akaev hosted a "Congress on the Importance of the Russian Language in the Community of the CIS" in Bishkek, only one month after the law had passed (SK 05/03/2004). In his opening-speech, Akaev stressed the avant-gardist role of the Russian language in the sphere of education and culture. Referring to his concept of "the common home," he stated that the "idea of the common home comprises the adaptation of Russian language as the language of inter-cultural communication," which was, in his view, closely intertwined with the process of Kyrgyzstan's democratization. "The Kyrgyz and the Russian language are to be understood as the left and the right hand of the same human body, though they are different, in every motion meant to support each other, they serve him in the same way" (ibid.).

3.2. Putin's New Russia and "The War on Terror"

Initially Russia and, to a certain extent, China, were the mainstays of Kyrgyz great power support. By 2002, this was expanded to a troika including the United States, when the regime saw fresh geopolitical vistas in the re-engagement of the U.S. in Central Asia following the terrorist attacks of 9/11 (Wood 2006: 8).

At the same time, Yeltsin's newly elected successor, Vladimir Putin, brought Central Asia back into mainstream Russian foreign policy thinking. To help justify Russia's reinvigorated security concerns in Central Asia, President Putin reminded the Central Asian leaders of not only Russia's historical ties to the region, but also its geographic position, permanently entwining Russia in security concerns of these states. The message was that although the United States is active in Central Asia now, "Russia will always be there, forever" (Bugubaev 2013: 5–6). Against this background, on July 27, 2000, Putin and Akaev signed two promising documents: First, a declaration of eternal friendship, unity (*soyuznichestvo*) and partnership, building upon the continuation and development of good neighborly, friendly relations in the 21st century. Second, a treaty about intensified economic cooperation between the two states (Rudov 2001: 314).

Two years later, in May of 2002, revelations concerning border transfers to China, which were based on a secret deal unapproved by Parliament, sparked an intense domestic scandal played out in the media, accompanied by political demonstrations and nation-wide protests. This had become further wrapped up in a domestic conflict, when the leader of the opposition "Asaba Party," Azimbek Beknazarov and his southern constituents initiated protests against the territorial settlement (Wood 2006: 29).

But Akaev was shown his limits when trying to justify his unilateral decision to concede land to China, using arbitrary interpretations of Kyrgyz history to legitimize his actions: Akaev, hinting at the military consequences of not reaching a settlement with China, portrayed the Chinese as ancient protectors of the Kyrgyz. Leaving aside for a moment the lessons of the Manas Epic, Akaev dug deeper into Central Asian history to commemorate a Chinese military victory in the Tien Shan in 751 against the advancing Arabs, a victory which allegedly saved the region from full integration into Middle Eastern civilization (Centrasia.ru 20/05/2002).

Citizens of Kyrgyzstan may argue among themselves whether their affinities are with Europe and the West, Russia and the CIS, Central Asia, or the Turkic or Islamic worlds. China, however, has not constituted such a reference point so far (Huskey 2006: 129). "If Akaev's words did little to endear China to the people of Kyrgyzstan, they certainly did nothing to enhance the president's reputation" (ibid. 30). On the contrary, they played into the hands of critics who saw an erosion of the country's sovereignty in the land transfer to China, the border realignments with Uzbekistan, and the accommodation of Western troops at the country's main airfield (Huskey 2006: 130). The persistent ambiguities in the national self-images Akaev delivered, which only reflected the contradictions inherent in his policies that those images were meant to portray as coordinated and coherent, clearly contributed to his downfall only three years later.

VI. The Second President: Kurmanbek Bakiev (2005–2010)

1. The Tulip Revolution

1.1. Kurmanbek Bakiev – A "Southerner" for President

The delegitimizing parliamentary elections of February and March 2005, taken together with a deepening economic crisis and a collapse of support for Akaev in particular in the southern half of the country, led to the overthrow of the Akaev regime and the installation of a consociational order: A president from the south, Kurmanbek Bakiev, assumed power in tandem with Felix Kulov as prime minister, who had been a northern opposition leader during Akaev's presidency (Huskey 2008: 12). This alliance enabled Bakiev to receive an overwhelming majority of roughly 90 percent of the vote in the July 2005 presidential elections. The forces that had driven the Tulip Revolution – independent business interests, informal networks and patronage ties – had developed under Akaev's 15-year rule and remained strong after his exit (Radnitz 2006: 132). Bakiev's decision to recognize the new, dubiously elected, and mostly pro-Akaev parliament on March 28, had almost surely prevented greater escalation (ibid. 140).

When President Bakiev settled into office in 2005, he developed a political system increasingly synonymous not only with him, but with his family, whose members he placed in charge of corporations and high posts within the state administration. In that sense, "The Bakiev regime developed a system which, in exchange for unquestioning loyalties, allowed key players near total impunity, and thus boundless opportunities for corruption" (ICG 2010: 5).

The new political power born of the "Tulip Revolution" of March 2005 had its main basis of support in the south, and, therefore, had to be built on a different legitimacy (Cummings & Ryabkov 2008: 243; Hale 2005). The southern elites saw in it a form of revenge on their political marginalization during the long reign of a northerner, Akaev (Laruelle 2012: 42). While, from a historical perspective, Bishkek and the north are supposed to have represented a more favorable attitude towards Russia, not least due to the concentration of the ethnic Russian minority in the north, the south had proven to be more nationalist, with growing tensions over business interest between Uzbek and Kyrgyz entrepreneurs at the time (Interview 18, 27/08/2014). In 2006, Kulov resigned as prime minister, and Bakiev's legitimacy, both symbolically (creating narrative) and pragmatically (creating consensus among elites), soon appeared to be based on a more ethno-centered Kyrgyz nationalism (Laruelle 2012: 42; Matveeva 2009: 1115–1117).

1.2. Russia and the Tulip Revolution: A Discourse of "Instability"

From Russia's perspective, having stability in the leadership of Kyrgyzstan is paramount, since it makes the relationship with this country predictable. But when regimes like Akaev's begin to focus above else on their regime's security, the relationship becomes counter-productive (Allison 2004: 284). President Putin had recently also been unhappy with Akaev's "fence sitting," preferring the Kyrgyz president to make a stronger and deeper commitment to Russia at the expense of the United States (Bernard 2005: 91–92). Therefore, the Kremlin sought contact with significant opposition members in order to preserve flexibility in conducting and implementing their regional strategy (Allison 2004: 286). President Putin's decision to host opposition leader and eventual interim President Kurmanbek Bakiev in January 2005, a week before Akaev visited Moscow was intended as an unambiguous message to Akaev and his regime (Bernard 2005: 92).

The close contact of Bakiev and other opposition members with Russia may have been the basis of the relative lack of concern in Moscow once it became clear that he would head the new government. In the first moment, the Russian and Chinese press implicated the West in the uprising and viewed it as a continuation of the wave of color revolutions that had swept across Georgia and Ukraine. It quickly became apparent, however, that Bakiev was not a Saakashvili or Yushchenko (Murzakulova 02/09/2014), and that the reasons for the Tulip Revolution lay in domestic discontent, most notably the political and economic marginalization of the southern half of the country throughout the 15 years of Akaev's rule (Huskey 2008: 12). Hence, in one of the first official Russian statements to be issued, on March 22, the chairman of the Duma Committee for CIS Affairs, Andrei Kokoshin, claimed that "this [was] a clash between the interests of various regional groups, which have always been there and which surface in critical moments" (as in CA-News.info 22/05/2005).

The role of ethnic minorities had constituted a point of contention between Kyrgyzstan and Russia since the early 1990s. Akaev desired to maintain and empower its Russian minority, even if not in political terms, and Russia supported this favorable treatment of its diaspora. But the events of March 2005 also suggested that a willingness by Moscow to intervene in Kyrgyz domestic politics to protect its citizens still existed. During the riots and looting in the wake of the parliamentary elections, some Russian individuals and enterprises were targeted by protestors. This brought the Russian Ambassador to publicly proclaim that there was a formal need to protect Russian citizens in Kyrgyzstan (Bernard 2005: 92). The return of Kulov, a non-Kyrgyz speaker and former head of the Kyrgyz security services, who seemed sympathetic to the needs of the Russian minority, was enough to stabilize the situation (Interview 3, 01/08/2014). However, the fact that the Russian Ambassador would openly call for Russian protection "[...] revalidated the latent power of the diaspora issue" (Bernard 2005: 92).

1.3. Bakiev's Answer: Kyrgyzstan Under the False Banner of "Internationalism"

When Kurmanbek Bakiev assumed power on March 25, 2005, he desired a new conception for Kyrgyzstan's foreign policy. The first statement concerning Kyrgyz post-revolution foreign policy was made by the acting foreign minister, Roza Otunbaeva, who said that "not only will there be no fundamental change in foreign policy, there will be no change at all in foreign policy" (VOA News 15/06/2005). In other words, Kyrgyzstan would keep on conducting Akaev's alleged "multi-vector" foreign policy (Nichol 2005: 3). This notion was reflected in Bakiev's initial identity rhetoric, aimed at appeasing Russia, Uzbekistan and the national minorities through strong emphasis on the internationalist agenda of the country's new leadership: "We are internationalists, and we don't want a disruption of our international community and nation (*obshchestva i naroda*)" (SK 05/04/2005; SK 01/03/2005).

While pretending that it pursued a foreign policy that is multi-vector in nature, the new Kyrgyz leadership had clearly chosen Russia as priority in the direction of its foreign policy (Chernov 2009). One of the first indications of this shift came as early as July 2005, shortly after a meeting of the Shanghai Cooperation Organization which requested that the United States set a deadline for the closing of its base in Kyrgyzstan (Huskey 2008: 12). During the same period, Bakiev made his first presidential visit to Russia and signed an agreement with Putin to increase military cooperation (Sari 2012: 142). The Kyrgyz ruling elites started emphasizing the great importance of Kyrgyz-Russian relations, supporting Bakiev's statements on their historical and cultural commonalities, the economic dependence of Kyrgyzstan, and the great potential of future developments of bilateral relations and cooperation (SK 21/06/2005; SK 05/09/2005; SK 08/09/2005).

However, already by the end of 2005, once the benevolence of the Russian community and, above all, the Russian state, seemed secured, Bakiev's rhetoric had become more specific on how the internal hierarchy of his "international community" would look like. Few days after his official inauguration as president on August 16, where he still addressed the nation with "Citizens of Kyrgyzstan and, Compatriots (*Kyrgyzstancy i Sootechestvenniki*) (SK 19/08/2005)," Bakiev gave a long speech in front of the state administration, where he referred to Kyrgyzstan as the ancient homeland of the great Kyrgyz people (*velikii narod kyrgyzov*), which had always found a place for its "friends" amongst them (SK 19/08/2005). This speech marked a subtle break with Akaev's identity rhetoric and politics, consequences of which shall be elucidated in the following paragraphs.

2. "The Discrepancy between Form and Content"

2.1. The *Ethnicization* of Kyrgyzstani Citizenship

On December 30, 2005, Bakiev signed a decree establishing a working group invested with a mission to elaborate "guidelines for the state and national ideology of Kyrgyzstan" (Marat 2008b: 46). In 2006, Adakhan Madumarov, State Secretary at the time, was appointed head of the commission in charge of developing "guidelines for a pan-national ideology" (*Kontseptsia obshchenatsional'noi ideologii*). But the guidelines were never published due to inability to forge consensus, and the commission was disbanded in 2009 during the institutional reforms to reinforce the power vertical (*vertikal' vlasti*) (Laruelle 2012: 42). After only one year in office, the increasing ethno-nationalist rhetoric of the Bakiev administration manifested itself in various legislative projects.

The new constitution, drafted after the ouster of President Akaev and approved on October 23, 2006, confirmed the status of Russian as an official language (Oruzbaev et al. 2008: 484). Nevertheless, Akaev's late attempts to upgrade the status of the state language continued to be upheld, as expressed in a law on citizenship passed in March 2007, making knowledge of Kyrgyz a condition for obtaining citizenship. The Ministry of Interior Affairs issued orders for all military personnel and hospital staff to learn Kyrgyz (Landau & Kellner-Heinkele 2011: 126). Subsequent legislation constituted a further step towards the *ethnicization* (Khan 2005) not only of politics, but of public life, too.

In November 2007, a large meeting of Russians living in Central Asia met in Kyrgyzstan to voice their grievances, which focused on what they saw as the downgrading of their language and culture. In order to conciliate the Russophones and meet the cultural demands of some ethnic Russian political groups (Knyazev 2008), early in 2008 the Ministry of Education and Science announced that a special program had been elaborated, aiming at promoting Kyrgyz-Russian bilingualism, acting both ways – promoting the teaching and study of Kyrgyz in Russian-medium schools while strengthening the position of Russian in the development of scientific research and in inter-state relationships (Landau & Kellner-Heinkele 2011: 129). However, the planned improvements never materialized.

Despite the lack of legislative support for conciliatory measures in the field of language policy and education, Bakiev's leadership soon resumed to promote a similar slogan to that of the Akaev era, "Kyrgyzstan – my homeland" (*Kyrgyzstan – moia rodina*), and called for more integrative conceptions of identity that should enhance "patriotism" among the Kyrgyzstani society (SK 29/09/2006; Fergananews.com 30/09/2009). Drawing on the memories of the Soviet experience, which already Akaev had identified a useful reference point (Matveeva 2009: 1101), the young generation was most targeted by these ideological temptations. Bakiev's elites suspected them of being the most "nihilistic" in terms of national identity, and the most influenced by "decadent" fashions from the West. In this, the same Soviet-inherited procedures used in Russia were employed such as, for example, getting higher secondary school pupils to write essays discussing the question of what state ideology should Kyrgyzstan have (Laruelle 2012: 42). Overall, popular identification with Sovietism was kept alive, had it yet never really gone away: common people in Kyrgyzstan continue to use Soviet-era place names instead of the official ones, Soviet holidays receive more attention than post-Soviet national holidays, and the late Soviet era is genuinely perceived as prosperous and harmonic (Interview 23, 09/09/2014; Matveeva 2009: 1105). One of the most noticeable examples of this nostalgia is the many statues and busts of Lenin in the public sphere as well as streets, schools, and places named after Lenin. While other former Soviet republics in Central Asia had statues of Lenin removed from central squares in the capital, Kyrgyzstan let them stay where they were (Cummings 2013: 609). Despite the fact that official rhetoric was increasingly leaning towards inclusive historical narratives again (Soviet past) during the last years of Bakiev's rule, there is only weak evidence for his intention to institutionalize such an inclusive, civic concept of national identity, that would have been reflected in adequate policies.

On the contrary, the president's amendments to the "Law on Television and Radio Broadcast" of April 24, 2008, even violated the new constitution, since it demanded that "more than half of the programs produced by TV and radio broadcaster should be conducted in the state language [Kyrgyz], at least 50% of the total amount of time must be covered with their own products and not less than 60% of the audiovisual contents presented should be provided by writers or performers from Kyrgyzstan" (Bishkek Press Club 17/09/2008). These laws hindered the development of multilingualism throughout the republic, and constituted a violation of paragraph 5.3 of the constitution, which states that "the Kyrgyz Republic guarantees all nationalities which constitute the people of Kyrgyzstan the right to preserve their mother tongue and create the conditions for learning and developing it" (Constitution of the Kyrgyz Republic, October 23, 2007).

According to Bakiev's views, there was an equal place for Kyrgyz as a national language and Russian as a language for communication with other members of the CIS (Landau & Kellner-Heinkele 2011: 129). With other members, however, he did not necessarily mean those residing within the borders of the Kyrgyz Republic.

In Kyrgyzstan, as Murzakulova & Dyatlenko (2012: 17) argue, language policy has rather been a state instrument to promote state ideology and national self-images in the first place, instead of serving as a tool for economic and social development. In that sense, aforementioned policies pursued under Bakiev should not necessarily be regarded as proof of a grand strategy to *kyrgyzify* the country's population. Those speeches and measures conveying internationalist and civic self-images, however, which had to a certain extent represented a viable alternative to ethno-nationalism under Akaev, slowly became transformed into merely a tool of (formal) appeasement. Internationalist rhetoric accompanied any new policy that limited minority rights and the use of non-titular languages, thus aiming to disguise these policies' discriminatory character. Had such a strategy not only failed to curtail fierce protests, it also encouraged the Russian and Uzbek intellectual elites to produce counter-narratives filling the void created by Bakiev's failure to offer cohesive ideological projects.

2.2. The Diasporas: Russian Self-defense and Increasing Uzbek Self-confidence

Throughout the five years of Bakiev's rule, Russia and its representatives in Bishkek used various occasions to draw attention to the worrying state of the Russian diaspora and its language. In December 2005, the KRSU hosted an international forum titled "21st Century – The Century of Intercultural Dialogue, Economic Prosperity and Spiritual Renaissance in the Eurasian Space," which highlighted the 125th anniversary of the inheritance of Russian education in Kyrgyzstan (DN 14/12/2005). Such events, Zheenbekov and a former advisor to the head of the Kyrgyz presidential administration argue, too often propagate a subtle imperialist message: Any attempt to upgrade the status of the Kyrgyz language and to foster the use of it is interpreted as a further move towards ethno-nationalism and a threat to Kyrgyzstan's multi-national, Soviet legacy. Such rhetoric tunes into the "neo-colonial discourse" that Russian media and the intellectual elite of Kyrgyzstan's ethnic Russians have allegedly created and that would discredit any attempt to establish the necessary foundation of a self-determined nation, keystone of which was a functioning titular language. Kyrgyzstan, they hold, is portrayed as fragile state, permanently on the verge of social and political collapse (Zheenbekov 18/08/2014; Interview 12, 15/08/2014).

In 2006, a new political party named *Sodruzhestvo* ("Concord") entered the political arena. The party's chairman became Vladimir Nifadev, who was also the director of the KRSU at the time (SK 23/02/2006). Presenting itself as a pragmatic, young and dynamic party, the program accentuated the fight against extremism, nationalism and the pursuit of an international community of friendship and harmony. Dual-citizenship and the guarantee of Russian as official language in the constitution were ought to be cornerstones of such a community (SK 06/04/2006). The party's links to the Russian political establishment became evident, when early in 2007 *Sodruzhestvo* and *Edinnaia Rossiia* ("United Russia") signed an agreement on close cooperation (24.kg 10/02/2007). Hence, even though not by official declaration, *Sodruzhestvo* was perceived by both Kyrgyz nationalists and the intellectual elite of Kyrgyzstan's ethnic Russians as a representative of the Russian diaspora's interests (Vremiia Vostoka 27/06/2012; Ivanov 14/09/2014). And, despite the fact that the party had no success in gathering many votes during the election, it could be perceived as the Slavonic minority's attempt to reclaim a niche in official Kyrgyzstani politics. According to Baisalov, Russia had allocated two million rubles in support of *Sodruzhestvo*, but "due to corruption, only about 100.000 eventually reached the party" (Baisalov 21/08/2014). However, even better funding would probably not have allowed for this "outsider" party to succeed in a system, where parties rather represent patronage networks than political ideas and an individual's identification with them (Interview 3, 01/08/2014). Already in 2007, *Sodruzhestvo* was merged into Bakiev's majority party (Ferganarews.ru 14/12/2007). After Bakiev's ouster in 2010, however, it re-appeared as independent party (Centralasiaonline.com 19/07/2010).

At the same time, also the Uzbek minority's political commitment had significantly increased since the "Tulip Revolution." While the broad mass of ethnic Russians in Kyrgyzstan has been widely perceived as apolitical, Uzbeks have proven to be more self-confident (Aytiev 14/08/2014; Ivanov 14/09/2014). Silent under Akaev and tacitly in favor of Bishkek, they had kept a low profile during the 2005 political struggles. The following year – for the first time since Uzgen in 1990 – the Uzbeks of Jalalabad poured out into the street to protest their absence of public recognition by the southern elites then in power. Growing "Uzbekophobia" among local law-enforcement agencies was another factor that united them against the elites in power (Laruelle

2012: 44). Politicians of Uzbek origin, disgruntled by official concessions to the much smaller Russian community, formed a National Cultural Center and voiced demands, among them the recognition of Uzbek as an official language and giving it its due in television programming and other cultural activities such as theatre productions and schooling (Omuralieva 2008: 44). At the same time, a new generation of younger Uzbek leaders emerged who had made a fortune in the private sector, such as Kadyrzhan Batyrov, and who wielded an even more aggressive discourse in terms of claims for the rights of the Uzbek minority (Fumagalli 2007b: 226; Khamidov 2006; Osmonov 2006). When in June 2006, Batyrov had taken up the issue of the Uzbek language again in parliament (*Zhogorku Kenesh*), Bakiev announced that he was rejecting the proposal to make Uzbek an official language, as he considered it potentially a destabilizing move (Landau & Kellner-Heinkele 2011: 134).

3. Bakiev's Downfall and the Russian Hand in the 2010 Revolution

Three years later, when Bakiev visited Moscow in February 2009, he signed a Russian financial assistance package, which included Russian debt-forgiveness, USD 300 million in low-interest credit loans and USD 1.7 billion for completing a hydroelectric power station. Furthermore, he declared that the in 2001 established American Transit Center at Manas airport will close, and asked the American military personnel to leave the country before the July 2009 presidential election in Kyrgyzstan (Eurasianet.org 02/02/2009). Such moves suggested Russia was enjoying unprecedented stature in the Kyrgyz leader's eyes. New agreements on the creation of joint plants, loans, and building hydro-energy stations on Kyrgyz territory further strengthened the ties between Kyrgyzstan and Russia (Sari 2012: 143; RIA Novosti 20/02/2008). However, following the July presidential election, Kyrgyz foreign policy shifted once again its attention to developing closer relations with the United States. Bakiev signed a new agreement with the United States to keep the military base at the airport under a different status, and, above all, with more payment of rent (Eurasianet 05/01/2012).

When Putin met with his Kyrgyz counterpart Prime Minister Danyar Usenov in early 2010, he accused Bakiev and his government of not keeping their promises (RFE/RL 23/02/2010; Sari 2012: 144). Once again, Bakiev's concerns over Russian support prompted him to draw on a Soviet narrative: On February 26, 2010, the Kyrgyz government celebrated the 85th anniversary of the establishment of the Soviet Kara-Kirghiz Autonomous Region (*Kara-Kirgizskaya Avtonomnaia Oblast'*) in 1924. During his address, Bakiev portrayed the USSR as the incubator of modern Kyrgyz statehood, thus indirectly lauding Russia, the union's former mother state (SK 26/02/2010). Even though this seems fairly accurate, argued from a historical perspective, Bakiev's narrative suggested a change from the idea of an ancient Kyrgyz nation, of which the undisputed founding father was the great Manas. Similar statements had preceded this occasion (SK 09/02/2010).

Despite Bakiev's efforts, Russian TV stations, which are popular in Kyrgyzstan, soon started to openly criticized Bakiev, and broadcast programs on the corruption of his family. The Russian government, previously refusing to talk with Kyrgyz opposition leaders, invited them to Moscow (Eurasianet.org 05/04/2010). On April 1, 2010, Russia terminated the preferred customs taxes that Kyrgyzstan had been enjoying. Prices of some products, especially oil and other products imported from Russia, increased and additionally provoked upheaval in the country (Sari 2010: 144). Bakiev and his closest relatives fled Bishkek on April 7, returning to their home town, Teyit, in southern Kyrgyzstan. From there, they tried in vain to regain support. Bakiev eventually fled the country and received asylum in Belarus (Rohde & Troels 2013: 43).

In the forefront to and during the upheaval, it had largely been Russian owned news outlets that created a particular narrative of the events and thus incited the anti-Bakiev campaign. A careful analysis of Kyrgyz and Central Asian media reports in the immediate aftermath of Bakiev's ouster reveals a circular flow of information between Kyrgyzstan and Russia, theoretical underpinnings of which were outlined in Chapter III.4.

Once again, the KRSU played a key role in this. During a round-table session on April 16, Alexander Knyazev proclaimed that the referendum on the interim government on July 27 was "the last chance for Kyrgyz statehood," (Rambler.ru 29.06.2010) and, continuing this "failed-state" discourse, concluded that "the titular ethnic group had failed to form the state of Kyrgyzstan" (Centrasia.ru 22/04/2010). Simultaneously, Russian language media, most of them owned by members of the Russo-Slavonic diaspora, constructed a threatening scenario of an allegedly emerging ethno-nationalism.

They highlighted violent acts of intimidation against national minorities, in particular Russians and Russian educational institutions, and even spoke of anti-Russian pogroms in some villages (Politkom.ru 15/04/2010; Centrasia. ru 15/04/2010; pr.kg 15/04/2010). The trustworthiness of the information provided is subject to fierce debate, and some Kyrgyz analysts and politicians even speak of an orchestrated campaign of disinformation (Nogoibaeva, 05/08/2014; Interview 12, 15/08/2014). The lack of verifiable information regarding the casualties these articles refer to, or official confirmation of deaths in the respective regions, make these reports seem even more doubtful. Interesting enough, is that the author of a large number of these articles was political scientist Larisa Choperskaya, the wife of the press attaché of the Russian Embassy in Bishkek, Vladimir Charchenko (Centrasia.ru 22/04/2010; Dieselelcat.kg 20/04/2010). The three above cited articles were published within two days only.

Immediately, those articles resounded from the heart of the Russian Federation's media landscape (Pravda.ru 19/04/2010) where the quotes of Choperskaya (Newsru.com 14/04/2010, Stoletie.ru 16/04/2010) and her allies reached eyes and ears of the Russian leadership. On April 19, the press-attaché of the Russian Embassy himself published a report in *Echo Moskvy*, that among the victims of the current turmoil in Kyrgyzstan were Russians (*russkie*) (as in Dieselelcat.kg 20/04/2010).

In response, the next day President Medvedev gave order to the Russian Ministry of Defense to protect lives and property of ethnic Russians in Kyrgyzstan (RBK 20/04/2010; BBC Russian-Service 20/04/2010), while referring to the worrying news reported by his press-attaché Charchenko and his wife Choperskaya to justify his decision.

The situation eased rapidly, due for the most part to a peaceful referendum in Kyrgyzstan that approved the interim-government under Roza Otunbaeva few days later. Nevertheless, the in this chapter elucidated circulation of narratives between Kyrgyzstan and Russia supports two assumptions: 1) The intellectual elite of the Russian diaspora in Kyrgyzstan has limited, but in some cases sufficient influence to shape the narrative of political events, and hence maintains influence on the overall identity discourse in the country; 2) Operating media and drawing on both formal and informal networks, the Russian diaspora's elites exert pressure on both the Russian Federation's leadership and the Kyrgyz government.

4. Identity Politics from Akaev to Bakiev: Between Persistence and Change

Bakiev's efforts to congeal a national identity for Kyrgyzstan retreated somewhat from the promotion of Kyrgyz culture via Manas and other ethnic symbols. In the footsteps of his predecessor, he continued Akaev's narrative of a "common home" of equals, cobbling together a concept of universalized, non-ethnic national identity that incorporated Kyrgyzstan's minority populations (Hanks 2011: 182–83).

Since the Tulip Revolution, the tools of reference available to elites and Kyrgyz society have barely evolved. The idea of the "friendship of peoples" and that of tolerance as a specific feature of Kyrgyz culture have been maintained. Claiming an ethnically pure state is not considered politically correct, while the dominant metaphor is that of a "common home" (Laruelle 2012: 43). While Akaev had still shown effort to institutionalize this self-image in his pursuit of a community of equal citizens, under Bakiev the relationship of peoples within this "home" shifted towards a hierarchy in ethno-nationalist fashion: The "common home" is shared by the "master of the house" and his "guests" (*khoziain/gost'*) (SK 19/08/2005). This metaphor implies that the guests must recognize that the landlord takes precedence when it comes to deciding cultural and social rules, and that he only accepts the guests thanks to his own good will (Laruelle 2012: 43). This notion was also reflected in Bakiev's legislation, which aimed at advantaging the ethnic Kyrgyz population and their language.

In sum, during the Bakiev era, the constitutive ambiguities of the Kyrgyz statehood have radicalized and the civic/ethnic balance has shifted in favor of the latter. Adakhan Madumarov did not hesitate to state that Kyrgyzstan was the state of the Kyrgyz people, one where, however, "minorities are welcome" (MSN.kg 31/07/2007). However, in moments of political instability, as in the immediate aftermath of the Tulip Revolution in 2005 on the one hand, and with anti-Bakiev protests gaining momentum towards the end of 2009, Bakiev employed an internationalist discourse of inter-ethnic harmony, drawing on inclusive historical narratives that were supposed to appease both minorities and Russia.

VII. The Third President: Roza Otunbaeva (2010–2011)

1. Another "Revolution"

1.1. The Pursuit of Stability

When on June 27, 2010, Roza Otunbaeva became confirmed by referendum as new interim president of the Kyrgyz Republic, she was the CIS's first female head of state. In March 2010, the democratic opposition had already formed an alternative "Popular Assembly," with Otunbaeva as head of its executive council. She had been foreign minister under Akaev, and had also served as the country's UN envoy to Georgia during the 2003 Rose Revolution there.

But Otunbaeva broke with Akaev in 2004 to join an opposition movement made up of former high-ranking establishment figures and supported the democratic mobilization in the Tulip Revolution (RFE/RL 08/04/2010). Also Bakiev had initially appointed her foreign minister, but she parted ways with him and joined the opposition SDPK party. For the split-prone opposition, Otunbaeva was a "clean" compromise choice for leader, as she was someone who was known for putting her commitment to democracy above personal ambition (Collins 2011: 154–55). After consultation with Prime Minister Usenov, Otunbaeva declared on April 7 that she was heading a provisional government, which had plans to draft a democratic constitution and hold elections within six months (Nichol 2010: 4). The referendum confirmed Otunbaeva as interim president until the end of 2011 and approved the constitution by an overwhelming 91 percent, based on a turnout nearing three-quarters of eligible voters. A presidential election was scheduled for late 2011, with Otunbaeva banned from running.

The new constitution put forward by the interim government represented the first serious attempt in the post-Soviet world to transform a strongly presidential system by limiting the powers of the presidency (Collins 2011: 157–58). It eliminated the presidential power of appointing governors and mayors – a major source of corruption and patronage (Nichol 2010: 6–7). Moreover, Otunbaeva used her powers as interim president to initiate a reform of the security agencies. The adoption of the new constitution paved the way for parliamentary elections in October 2010. Even though the interim-government had dissolved Bakiev's old ruling party, it allowed a new party aligned with the ex-president (Ata-Zhurt) to register along with more than hundred others. The balloting was the first truly competitive and unpredictable election in Kyrgyzstan's history (Zheenbekov 18/08/14; Collins 2011: 158).

1.2. Russia and the Interim-Government

In stark contrast to his labeling the ouster of Akaev as "illegitimate" five years earlier, Russian Prime Minister Vladimir Putin became the first foreign leader to offer support to Kyrgyzstan's interim government when he telephoned Otunbaeva on April 8, one day after Bakiev had fled the capital. By April 14, Russia had already pledged USD 20 million in humanitarian aid and a USD 30 million loan at a reduced interest rate to Kyrgyzstan (Bohr 2010: 3). The Kremlin's immediate offer of aid to the provisional government in Kyrgyzstan came as a surprise, prompting some observers to speculate that Moscow had instigated the violent ouster of the Bakiev government (ibid. 4; Nichol 2010: 8).

The United States, on the contrary, showed great caution. In an interview with CNN a few days after the revolt, Otunbaeva criticized "the United States [for not being] interested in our [Kyrgyzstan's] democratic development, with what was going on within the country [...] For you [the US] we understand that the base is a high priority, and you focused only on the base" (CNN 14/06/2010). At the same time as she expressed her anger with the United States for not having concerned itself with the predicament of the opposition during Bakiev's rule (Bohr 2013: 5), Otunbaeva expressed her gratitude towards Moscow for its "support in exposing the family of a nepotistic, criminal regime" (Reuters 08/04/2010). Only after she had suggested that there would be no change in the status of the Manas base did Assistant Secretary of State Robert Blake visit Bishkek and offer Washington's help. That was one week after the revolution.

However, even though Russia was initially overjoyed at the turn of events in Kyrgyzstan, later developments were decidedly less satisfactory for the Kremlin. The American military base was kept, and the interim government moved to rebuild its legitimacy by restoring democratic institutions wrecked by Bakiev (Wu 2011: 72).

1.3. The June Events

Political and social tensions remained high after the April Revolution. In June 2010, the most serious ethnic conflict in 20 years erupted in the Kyrgyz part of the Fergana Valley, with 2,000 deaths and more wounded, mostly Uzbeks (ICG 2012). The riots broke out after Bakiev fled to Belarus, leaving his followers in the south agitated and angry. Ethnic relations between the majority Kyrgyz and the minority Uzbeks had worsened under Bakiev's rule, with fierce competition over resources aggravated by declining remittances from the migrant workers to the North gaining momentum (Collins 2011: 160). The severe conflict between forces for and against Bakiev brought further confusion and disturbance to the fragile social equilibrium of the south. With the interim government unable to control the situation, it called on Russia for help (Wu 2010: 73–74).

Assignment of responsibility for the 2010 events is beyond the scope of this book. However, it is clear that the outcome of the violence and the post-violence reconstruction has been to diminish Uzbek influence and, at least symbolically, to proclaim the south as Kyrgyz territory (ICG 2012). Regardless of how we interpret the causes of the 2010 June events, it is undeniable that the south is currently being *kyrgyzified*, and that, at present, "Uzbeks are losing ground in the symbolic, economic, and cultural spheres" (Wachtel 2013: 879; RFE/RL 08/06/2011).

2. The Dialectics of National Identity and Foreign Policy Reconsidered: The Demise of the "Common Home"

2.1. A New Foreign Policy

The lack of a central foreign policy director was a genuinely new experience for Kyrgyzstan. In the arguably authoritarian regimes of previous presidents Askar Akaev and Kurmanbek Bakiev, foreign policy had fallen almost exclusively under the presidential domain (Marat 2011). After Bakiev's ouster, the country's major political players were unable to agree upon the country's new foreign policy priorities: While Prime Minister Almazbek

Atambaev and his deputy, Omurbek Babanov, seemed keen to join the Russian-led Customs Union, Otunbaeva warned that it was too early for Kyrgyzstan to take such a step. Furthermore, when Finnish diplomat, Kimmo Kiljunen, who headed the international investigation into the violence in Kyrgyzstan in June 2010, was banned from entering the country by parliament, the president called on Members of Parliament to reconsider their decision (Kabar.kg 24/06/2011). Eventually, it was Kyrgyzstan's Foreign Minister Ruslan Kazakbaev whose voice served as a blend of parliament, prime minister, as well as the president's policies. Kazakbaev defended the parliament's decision to ban Kiljunen, praised the importance of cooperation with Moscow, and expressed hope that US-Kyrgyz relations continue to prosper (Marat 2011; RFE/RL 06/04/2012).

The new constitution signified a break with Kyrgyzstan's tradition of almost undisputed foreign policy authority exercised by the president. A wide range of competing ideas of how the country's national interest was to be defined shaped the debates at the highest echelon of power as never before. Definitions of national interest indicate a hierarchy of foreign policy partners. In turn, relationships with foreign countries serve to reinforce or undermine the legitimacy of different national self-images. They can determine whether these images are viewed as historically legitimate and effective, or not (Clunan 2009: 44–45). Hence, the gradual disintegration of interpretive authority in the context of the country's national interest and identity after the 2010 revolution ushered in a new era of identity discourse in Kyrgyzstan, making it more open and competitive than ever before.

2.2. Manas Conquers the "Common Home"

Bakiev's overthrow in April 2010 reopened public debate on the nature of the Kyrgyz political regime (Temirkulov 2010: 597), and the events of June revived public discussions on the Kyrgyz state and its national identity (Laruelle 2012: 45). As in 2005, the country's leadership had to determine whether the concepts of national self-images promoted prior to the revolution were still "realistic," that is, effective or practical guides for the state, given the prevailing international and domestic conditions the country faces and its historical aspirations (Clunan 2009: 7–8). However, as established earlier, the new constitutional limits to the presidential power opened the identity debate to a wider range of political actors who promoted alternative images of Kyrgyzstan's national-self.

Additionally, the ambivalence that many of the slogans and symbols had acquired under Akaev and Bakiev further complicated the task of post-revolution nation-building. An example is the ambiguous use of the term "patriotism," which had become a substantial part of the Bakiev administration's civic concept of a national identity. The term "patriot" has today come to take on such a large variety of meanings that the message of identity that it intends to convey is almost inaudible: depending on the group or groups involved, patriotism is presented either as a civic identity opposing the rise of ethno-nationalism, or as a political expression of ethno-nationalism (Laruelle 2012: 45). For instance, in order to assure the security of goods and persons during the events of spring 2010, a voluntary patriotic militia, the DND Patriot, formed and participated in securing public spaces alongside the police (rdf.in.kg, 03/08/2010). Since the legislative elections of October 2010, the supporters of Roza Otunbaeva had called for citizens to begin a patriotic surge and prevent the country from sinking into civil war. Groups of young activists, such as the movement "My – Kyrgyzstancy!," have referred to civic patriotism in order to overcome ethnic divisions among the youth, drawing on an updated rhetoric of the "friendship of peoples" (Laruelle 2012: 45).

Aforementioned groups use patriotism to oppose nationalism. At the same time, however, the term patriotism dominated among those political forces that promoted an ethno-nationalist agenda. This was the case with the high-profile *Ata-Zhurt* ("Fatherland") party, which collected close to nine percent of the vote at the legislative elections of October 2010, thus receiving more seats than any other party. The party has mainly been run by politicians from the south close to the Bakiev elites (ibid.).

Ata-Zhurt accused Otunbaeva's government of setting up the country's future in a way that would not suit the "mentality" of the Kyrgyz people and that was not based on their history as a nation. The party further emphasized the unique antiquity of the Kyrgyz people, and called for a better structured patriotic education of Kyrgyzstan's youth (Fergananews. ru 28/01/2011). However, Tashiev's popular success had never been based on a sophisticated ideological program. He rather took up simple notions considered as consensual among the population: "The titular nation must be superior; it cannot be inferior to the other ethnicities in the country. The latter must respect our tradition, our language, our history, and then everyone will live in peace" (Fergananews.ru 16/09/2010).

On the official administrative-level, the framework for civic concepts of national identity still existed. A constitution and laws that refer to equality for all ethnic groups, stating that no one may be discriminated against on the basis of ethnicity and that all are allowed to determine their own ethnicity (Constitution of the Kyrgyz Republic, June 27, 2010). A number of institutions with the official goal of improving ethnic relations, such as the Peoples' Assembly, hadn't been disbanded, and Soviet symbols continued to be embraced officially.

In that sense, on the occasion of the 70th anniversary of the beginning of the Great Patriotic War, Prime Minister Atambaev called on the population of Kyrgyzstan to focus on the glorious heritage it shares with Russia and the whole of the CIS states. Forgetting this common memory would bestow the cursed fate of a *mankurt* upon the peoples of Kyrgyzstan. Thus Atambaev linked his view of Kyrgyzstan's past unequivocally with its foreign policy, creating a national self-image that was both historically legitimate and reflected Kyrgyzstan's foreign policy priorities. Based on the memory of a common past, a common future ought to be built: "Kyrgyzstan's main strategic partner today is Russia" (SK 23/06/2011).

Atambaev's use of the *mankurt*-metaphor was, however, unprecedented in such a context: In Central Asian lore, *mankurts* were prisoners of war whose willpower and memory of past events and even of their parents had been taken away by a torturous process of brainwashing. In 1980, famous Kyrgyz writer Chyngyz Aitmatov made the mankurts' destiny a leitmotif of his novel *The Day Lasts More Than a Hundred Years*. Throughout the Soviet Union, the term *mankurtism* was soon widely used as a synonym for the brutal way in which the Soviet people had been cut off from their historical memory as the result of a radical and totalitarian identity policy (Horton & Brashinsky 1992: 131). Towards this background, Atambaev used the metaphor to glorify the period of history it was originally supposed to condemn, flipping its essential meaning. Thus, he manipulated a popular metaphor that had its roots in the ethnic Kyrgyz nationalist movement to use it as part of a civic self-image of Kyrgyzstan, deeply entrenched in its "glorious" Soviet past. In fact, this example is the indicator of a tendency that already had transpired under Bakiev: the use of certain symbols in both the construction of civic and ethnic defined national self-images. The double-identity thus attained by one and the same symbol, or, in this case, historical narrative and metaphor, does not reinforce its symbolic power, but, on the contrary, neutralizes it.

The year 2011 had begun with a more elegant attempt by president Otunbaeva to compromise the message of the country's ethnic-Kyrgyz tradition on the one hand, with one that at the same time recognizes Russia as political hegemon. In accordance with a decree signed by Otunbaeva on December 28, 2010, the year 2011 was declared the "Year of Kurmanzhan-Datka" in Kyrgyzstan in honor of the 200th anniversary of her birth (SK 21/01/2011). Kurmanzhan-Datka is an unusual figure in Central Asian history. Born in the Kokand Khanate (centered in the Ferghana Valley, covering parts of modern-day Uzbekistan and southern Kyrgyzstan) in 1811, her decision to flee her betrothed for an influential feudal lord, for instance, has seen her championed by modern day campaigners against bride kidnapping. On her husband's death, she was acknowledged as ruler of the Alai Mountains. She later followed other Kyrgyz clan leaders in accepting Russian military superiority as Tsarist armies marched south. When her son was subsequently arrested by Tsarist officers for smuggling, she accepted her son's execution rather than risk St. Petersburg's wrath by rebelling (Eurasianet.org 20/08/2013). Thus, Kurmanjan Datka could be interpreted as a historical figure that compromises the acceptance of Russia's dominating role in Central Asia with an accentuation of a clearly ethno-centered historical narrative of the country.

However, Otunbaeva's government was also constructing ethnic defined self-visions of the state that were intended to appeal solely to the titular nation. Since the Ata-Zhurt party was gathering huge amounts of votes with their radical nationalist agenda, and the June events had split the country into "victims" and "perpetrators," the ruling elite more than ever had to rely on a Kyrgyz-centered legitimacy. A month after the Osh riots, Otunbaeva requested that Manas be included in the school curricula (SK 25/02/2011), "probably in order to prevent southern politicians from hijacking the attributes of *Kyrgyzness* that are linked to the figure of Manas for themselves" (Laruelle 2012: 45). During her speech on the 20th anniversary of the Kyrgyz Republic's independence day, Otunbaeva referred to

Manas as "most powerful, most attractive, and unifying symbol of our being, the source of our [Kyrgyzstan's], spiritual strength, moral grandeur, and an example of the unselfishness and self-sacrifice" (Otunbaeva 31/08/2011). For this reason, Otunbaeva further argued, the spirit of Manas must constantly be revived, "which can make it possible for each one [...] and for the whole to be capable of a real feat in work, heroism and benevolence as did [...] Aikol Manas - Manas the Benevolent" (ibid.). Unlike Akaev, Otunbaeva didn't bother to underline the cosmopolitan character of Manas.

In what is most likely the largest public art project of the post-Soviet period in Kyrgyzstan, the Osh municipality has erected a number of eye-catching monuments at strategic points in the city. All of them are dedicated to Kyrgyz heroes from various epochs, thereby ignoring the co-presence of Uzbeks and other minorities in the city. Even a project seemingly as ecumenical as the "peace bell," which was unveiled in Osh on the second anniversary of the June 2010 "events," was inscribed without any reference to Uzbek culture (the inscription is in English, Russian, and Kyrgyz) (Wachtel 2013: 980). The radical nationalist sentiments and policies growing in the Kyrgyz south after the June events reinforced the political north-south divide of the country. They forced the government in Bishkek to constantly react to their claims, and to consider them when attempting to design new national self-images. If Roza Otunbaeva regularly denounced the risk of new inter-ethnic clashes and the radicalization of the youth, the members of her government could not condemn the wave of Kyrgyz nationalism on which they base their social legitimacy. They therefore could not criticize the Kyrgyz perpetrators, sack the security forces that had refused to restore order in Osh, or protect the Uzbek minority. Neither could they admit that they had enjoyed the support of Uzbek leaders like Batyrov in their campaign against Bakiev, without incurring a major loss of legitimacy among the ethnic majority (Laruelle 2012: 47).

The idea that the Uzbeks were primarily responsible for the Osh conflict has gained considerable acceptance in Kyrgyzstan (ibid. 46; The New York Times 02/07/2010; RFE/RL 08/06/2011). They are accused of having grown wealthy off the backs of the pauperized Kyrgyz, and their demands for linguistic recognition and political rights are heard as an indirect call for independence with the aim to destroy Kyrgyzstan's unity.

During the interim presidency of Roza Otunbaeva, a Department of Inter-Ethnic Relations, Religious Policies and Interaction with Civil Society was established in the President's Office. It analyzed and compiled the findings and recommendations of the various national and international reports on the Osh violence, and produced a "concept of ethnic policy and consolidation" entitled "Kyrgyzstan is my homeland," plus an action plan on their implementation, which was comprehensive in coverage but vague in terms of responsibility and funding sources (RFE/RL 18/06/2011). It spotlighted a commitment to Kyrgyzstan as a "multilingual" and "multicultural" society, in which "the creation of conditions for the study and development of minority languages was guaranteed, and any discrimination by failure to know state and official languages [was] to be sanctioned" (Concept of Ethnic Policy and Consolidation; Megoran 2012: 21). The strong focus of the concept on language, however, and the absence of the issue of representation in the state service once again reflected the discrepancy between form and content of state sponsored civic nationalism, already observed in both the Akaev and Bakiev periods (Interview 26, 11/09/2014; Doolotkeldieva 14/08/2014).

Projects like the new concept of inter-ethnic relations have been strongly supported by the OSCE High Commissioner on National Minorities, the OSCE Centre in Bishkek and the office of the United Nations High Commissioner for Human Rights, which had repeatedly called for the construction of a civic nation (Kabar.kg 17/02/2011). Therefore, scholars like Andrew Wachtel, current president of the American University of Central Asia, argue that it was neither Russia nor its diaspora that has been successful in promoting civic values and contained a stronger state-sponsored ethno-nationalist agenda. Rather, it was the presence and pressure of international organizations and Western powers, the Kyrgyz government had to give in to (Wachtel 12/08/2014). However, the question remains to what extent such imported ideas of a "modern" civic identity promoted by these organizations can actually complement or reinforce those civic concepts promoted by the government. So far, neither those drawing on the common Soviet past, nor those presented as example of modern "civic nations" have been effectively transformed into respective institutional frameworks. Interesting to note, the consensus amongst the officials at the State Department for Inter-Ethnic Relations seems to be, that inter-ethnic relations during Soviet times had been overall harmonious and well organized (Interview 6, 05/08/2014).

It is first and foremost this historical narrative, for which the major reference point is still Russia, rather than the U.S. or other Western dominated organizations, that keeps the vision of a multi-ethnic "home" alive.

After 2010, more stakeholders were involved in the process of official identity construction, which made it more difficult for the elites to reach consensus on appropriate self-images. This also meant, that self-images were much faster discarded or re-modeled, as, unlike under Akaev or Bakiev, the opposition had more power to mobilize public support in order to discredit these images' legitimacy, and more platforms to offer their own. At the same time, the domestic dimension of identity politics seemed to have gained priority, once the external environment appeared favorable to the interim-government, and Russia's support was secured.

2.3. The Fourth President and the Eurasian Vector

In December 2011, Almazbek Atambaev was elected the fourth president of the Kyrgyz Republic, and with him a whole new dimension of Kyrgyzstan's identity discourse appeared on the horizon. A variety of new variables were introduced that added to the complexity of Russo-Kyrgyz relations, consideration of which would have exceeded the scope of the present analysis. In the context of Putin's re-election in 2012, an ever stronger anti-western counter-narrative was being projected upon Russia's "near abroad" (Sergunin & Karabeshkin 2015; Umland 2012: 2–3; Komersant 07/04/2012). And while Otunbaeva's administration had mostly been expressing doubts on whether to join Putin's project of a Eurasian Economic Union, a more polarized discourse unfolded once Atambaev had taken over. In addition, several new Russian organizations, among them *Russotrudnichestvo*, entered the stage, the mission and impact of which are yet to be understood. Though Atambaev's speeches have attempted to strike a balance between ethno-nationalist and internationalist portrays of the country, his administration has further pushed the *ethnicization* of public life, along with discriminatory language and education policies that hit the Uzbek minority particularly hard (RFE/RL 13/03/2014; HRW World Report 2014; Wachtel 12/08/13). But while some observers lament on Russia's lack of interest for Kyrgyzstan's reinforced ethno-nationalist policies, and its reluctance to defend its stricken diaspora (Ivanov 14/09/2014; Uchkempirov 08/08/2014), many Kyrgyz intellectuals and politicians remain skeptical regarding Russia's strong grip on the small country, and see this strong dependence reflected in the country's desperate pursuit of a national identity (Zheenbekov 18/08/2014; Murzakulova, A. 02/09/2014; Interview 12, 15/08/2014). During the revelation ceremony of a Manas Statue in Moscow's Park of Friendship in 2012, Atambaev, to the dismay of many Kyrgyz historians (Chorotegin 08/09/2014), claimed that the epic hero Manas had also Russian origins (*rossianin*). The debate is anything, but close to an end.

Conclusion

The present study has examined the causes of the constant variations between civic and ethnic concepts of national identity in the official rhetoric of the Kyrgyz leadership between 1991 and 2012. It has further shed light on the interrelationship between the country's official identity discourse and the policies that were intended to regulate the country's inter-ethnic relations. Although Kyrgyzstan's pursuit of a national identity has been researched in the past, scholars have mainly emphasized domestic drivers when explaining the use of rhetoric and symbols by the country's leadership and elites. This book, on the contrary, illuminated the international dimension of Kyrgyzstan's identity formation. Kyrgyzstan's leadership, according to this study's first hypothesis, has to maintain a delicate balance of tensions created and conditioned by domestic and foreign policy challenges. In order to address these challenges simultaneously, Kyrgyz leaders have shifted between civic and ethnic defined concepts when offering visions of Kyrgyzstan's national identity that would legitimize their policies in front of domestic and international audience. While ethnic concepts of national identity have been deployed strategically to appeal to the ethnic Kyrgyz population and rally them around the state, civic concepts of national identity have been used to appease minorities and international donors. This observation reaffirms the explanatory value of Aspirational Constructivism, through which one can conclude that Kyrgyz leaders define the national interest and identity inspired by common historical memories and current socio-political challenges in an attempt to integrate Kyrgyzstan's international and domestic realms.

In the early 1990s, the slogan "Kyrgyzstan – our common home" was supposed to foretell the country's new identity, with Kyrgyzstan as civic nation encompassing and superseding all ethnic affiliations. The memory of the Soviet past nurtured the civic national self-image of Kyrgyzstan, while the Soviet double-identity concept was intended to function within one country only.

This idea of a civic nation had first and foremost been deployed to consolidate the Kyrgyzstani society in the aftermath of the Osh riots (1990), and, to prevent further emigration of the Slavonic population, which had been driven out in part by fear of policies privileging the titular nation. The "Silk Route Doctrine" was meant to unify the divergent strings of Akaev's previous identity rhetoric, and to simultaneously portray the country's multi-vector foreign policy as a reflection of the multi-national character of the Kyrgyzstani society. Kyrgyzstan's strong dependence on Russia as donor and security provider was another reason for Akaev to put forth and maintain a primarily civic image of the nation throughout the 15 years of his reign. Following Aspirational Constructivism, leaders also test and adjust identity and interests in response to external events or as reflection of current foreign policy orientations; this is how stable national identities are altered and modified, and this is why Akaev's rhetoric drew on self-images appealing to Russia and "its" minority. In practice, however, Akaev's civic-based ideas and institutions were not as successful and persuasive as they were to have been in theory. Domestic variables, such as the brutal social transformations, and in particular the rural exodus of the Kyrgyz, made it necessary to assure the promotion of the titular nationality in order to guarantee social peace (Laruelle 2012: 41). Furthermore, Akaev was facing increasing oppositional pressure by the mid-1990s, and so, in order to consolidate his voters prior to the elections of 1995, shifted the focus of his ideology from the "common home" to a more ethno-centered national self-image, represented in the epic of Manas. The double identity narrative of the Kyrgyz state, and especially the civic component of it, became gradually more disconnected from the social and political evolutions of the country during the late 1990s and the early 2000s (ibid.)

Even if the step to acknowledge Russian as official language had been seen as a step towards a civic nation, the "Batken events," and increasing regime insecurity provoked a return to further ethno-nationalism. By the third term of Akaev's presidency, the deployment of civic self-images appeared to be solely instrumental, and the excessive ambiguity in the use of the various slogans and symbols undermined their appeal to the various parts of society.

During the Bakiev era, the constitutive ambiguities of Kyrgyz statehood eventually altered the civic-ethnic balance in favor of the latter: While Akaev still made a demonstrated effort to institutionalize a civic self-image in pursuit of a community of equal citizens, the relationship of peoples within the allegoric "common home" (*obshchii dom*) had shifted under Bakiev towards a hierarchy in ethno-nationalist fashion: The "common home" is shared by the "master of the house" and his "guests." However, in moments of political instability, i.e. whenever an intervention on behalf of Russia seemed likely, whether in the immediate aftermath of the Tulip Revolution in 2005, or with anti-Bakiev protests gaining momentum towards the end of 2010, Bakiev employed an internationalist discourse of inter-ethnic harmony, drawing on inclusive historical narratives that were supposed to appease both national minorities and Russia.

The second hypothesis of this study claimed that the promotion of a civic understanding of the national-self should not only be considered a result of Kyrgyz leadership's passive "self-censorship" of discriminatory policies that might displease Russia. Such rhetoric has been used to accommodate the Russian diaspora's complaints and to respond to its active commitment to countering ethno-nationalist views and policies promoted by the government. Indeed, despite their exclusion from political power structures, the Russian diaspora's elite in Kyrgyzstan wielded limited, but in some cases remarkable influence on the narrative of political events, and hence had (and has) influence on the overall discourse in the country. Moreover, Russian organizations and institutions such as the KRSU, offered counter-narratives to ethno-nationalist rhetoric, emphasizing common legacies and the strong role Russia played and still needed to play in Kyrgyzstan. Operating media and drawing on both formal and informal networks, the Russian diaspora's elites exert pressure on both the Russian Federation's leadership and the Kyrgyz government.

Even so, it is perhaps more accurate to speak of certain active interest groups, rather than a "diaspora" with a coherent identity as such. The lack of coordination, funding and an overarching organizational framework makes Russian activists like Alexandr Ivanov, currently president of the Russian Unifying Union of Compatriots (ROSS), speak in increasingly pessimistic terms about Kyrgyzstan's future as multi-ethnic state (Ivanov 14/09/2014). In addition, the demographic situation has changed in the titular nation's favor: By 2009, the ethnic Kyrgyz population had already comprised approximately 70% of citizens, with the non-Asian, non-Muslim populations having dropped from some 36% in 1989 to approximately 8.5% (as in Wachtel 2013: 974). However, assessing the diaspora's impact also requires asking whether Russia has ever been prepared to intervene for the right of its "compatriots" in Kyrgyzstan, who are those immediately affected by Kyrgyz ethno nationalism. The evidence is rather poor. For this reason, one might argue that Russia accepts ethno-nationalist state building in return for Kyrgyztan's policy alignment. Indeed, in the face of thousands of Kyrgyz migrant workers in Russia currently feeding their relatives in Kyrgyzstan, and the country's ever growing security dependency on Russia, the Kremlin has had no need to develop its soft-power tools in Kyrgyzstan. But the past three years have brought many changes regarding both Russia's technical and ideational approach towards it's new abroad, and the future role of the many Russian "NGOs" that have appeared lately cannot be clearly foreseen. Further research would be necessary in that context.

After the revolution of 2010, the disintegration of the interpretive authority over Kyrgyzstan's national interest and identity allowed for an identity discourse more open and competitive than ever before. The interim-president Otunbaeva knew how to please both Russia and the international community with her rhetorical choices, as evidence in both historical narrative and policy drafts, such as the 2011 concept on intern-ethnic relations. At the same time, one might infer that the repeated absence of Russian direct interference in 2010 resulted in a revival of Akaev's Manas cult after the "June events," even though in parts this revival was surely necessitated by the strong southern opposition under the Ata-Zhurt party's leadership. However, some scholars interpret the reinforced emphasis on ethno-nationalism differently. They argue that Kyrgyzstan has been teleologically drifting towards the ethno-national concept of nationhood, for the route to all modern state consolidation has been through ethno-national consolidation.[5] Moreover, there is no example of an ethno-national state that created positive conditions for minorities until it completed its democratic transition (and until the percentage of minorities fell below approximately 15%)

---

5   "A state of citizens, liberal and individualistic, in which ethnic identity was subordinate to an abstract civic identity has never successfully occurred outside the Anglo-American world, and even there it has occurred primarily in those states (USA, Canada, New Zealand, and Australia) in which the original inhabitants were almost completely eliminated and replaced by immigrants who could not claim deep historical ties to the land" (Wachtel 2013: 972).

(Wachtel 2013). Against this background, this book still provided evidence for how Kyrgyzstan's geographical, historical and political proximity to and dependence from Russia has slowed the process of ethno-national state and nation-building substantially.

After all, it is important to note that Russia is not the only international variable on which the fate of Kyrgyzstan's nation-building process depends on. While Uzbekistan has served as an important "other" in Kyrgyzstan's public identity discourse, president Karimov's open distrust and ignorance (Fumagalli 2007b) towards the Uzbek diaspora has granted Kyrgyz statesmen a "free hand" when excluding Uzbeks systematically, successfully ignoring their cultural ties with the country when speaking of Kyrgyzstan's national identity. However, if once the Uzbek leadership took on a more aggressive stance towards their small neighbor, or showed an active interest in its diaspora, the ethno-nationalist "teleology" of Kyrgyzstan's nation-building process might be challenged anew, once again re-opening the question that this book has tried to answer.

Bibliography

Adamson, F. & Demetriou, M. (2007) "Remapping the Boundaries of 'State' and 'National Identity:' Incorporating Diasporas into IR Theorizing," *European Journal of International Relations* 13.4, 489–526.

Akaev, A. (1992a) "Contribution to Russian Recovery," as published in: *Daily Report. Central Eurasia, Moscow INTERFAX – 15 July 1992*, FBIS-SOV-92–138 on 17 July 1992.

Akaev, A. (1992b) Interviewed on "Live Dialogue," Ostankino Television First Program in Russian, 1125 GMT, 24 May 1992, translated in FBIS-SOV 92–104 (29 May 1992), p. 60.

Akaev, A. (1998) *Otkrovennyi razgovor [Frank Conversation]*, Moscow: Sovershenno Sekretno.

Akaev, A. (2002) *Trudnaia doroga k demokratii [Difficult Road to Democracy]*, Moscow: Mezhdunarodnye otnosheniia.

Akaev, A. (2004) *Dumaia o budushem s optimizmom [Thinking about the future with optimism]*, Moscow: Mezhdunarodnye otnosheniia.

Akaev, A. (2004) *Kyrgyzskaya gosudarstvennost' i narodnyi epos "Manas" [Kyrgyz statehood and the national epic of Manas]*, Bishkek: Raritet.

Akaev, A. (2004) *The Diplomacy of the Silk Road (A Foreign Policy Doctrine)*, New York: Global Scholarly Publications.

Akcali, P. & Engin-Demir, C. (2013) *Politics, Identity and Education in Central Asia: Post-Soviet Kyrgyzstan*, London: Routledge.

Allison, R. (2004) "Strategic Reassertion in Russia's Central Asia Policy," *International Affairs* 80.2, 277–293.

Almakuchukov, K. (2010) *Kul'turnaia Politika v Kyrgyzstane: Metod Issledovaniia I analiza gosudarstvennoi politiki (compendium) [Cultural Politics in Kyrgyzstan: Research Methods and Analysis of state politics]*, Bishkek: Mara.

Alonso, A. (1994) "The Politics of Space, Time and Substance: State Formation, Nationalism, Ethnicity," *Annual Review of Anthropology* 23, pp. 379–405.

Alter, P. (1994) *Nationalism*, 2nd Edition, London: Edward Arnold.

Aminov, K., Jensen, V., Juraev, S., Overland, D. Tyan, D., Ulu, Y. (2010) "Language Use and Language Policy in Central Asia," *Central Asia Regional Data Review*, 2.1:, retrieved 22/01/2015.

Amrekulov, N. & Masanov, N. (1994) *Kazakhstan mezhdu proshlym I budushim samosoznania [Kazakhstan between past and future self-consciousness]*, Almaty: Beren.

Anderson, J. (1997) *The International Politics of Central Asia, Regional International Politics*. Manchester: Manchester University Press.

Anderson, J. (1999) *Kyrgyzstan: Central Asia's Island of Democracy?*, Post-communist States and Nations. Amsterdam: Harwood Academic.

Asankanov, A. (1997) *Kyrgyzy: rost natsional'nogo samosoznania [The Kyrgyz: the rise of national self-consciousness]*, Bishkek: Muras.

Bakhtin, M. (1981) "Discourse in the Novel," in: Holquist, M. (ed.) *The Dialogic Imagination*, Austin: University of Texas Press), p. 360–61.

Bandura, A. (1977) "Self-Efficacy: Toward a Unifying Theory of Behavioral Change," *Psychological Review*.

Baran, Z. (2007) "EU energy security: time to end Russian leverage," *The Washington Quarterly*, 30.4, 131–144.

Benningsen, A. & Broxup, M. (1983) *The Islamic Threat to the Soviet State*, London: Croom Helm.

Berdikeeva, S. (2006) "National Identity in Kyrgyzstan: The Case of Clan Politics," *Eurasia21*: http://www.aytmatov.org/metinler/national_identity_of_kyrgyzstan_the_case_of_clan_politics.pdf, retrieved April 2, 2014.

Bernard, A. (2005) "The Eagle, The Bear and the Yurt: Evaluating Kyrgyzstan's Foreign Policy Behavior With the United States and Russia in the Post-9/11 Security Environment," Master Thesis at the Naval Postgraduate School Monterey, California.

Billing, M. (1995) *Banal Nationalism*, London: Sage Publications.

Bingol, Y. (2010) "Nationalism and democracy in post-communist Central Asia," in: *Asian Ethnicity*, 5.1, 43–60.

Blagov, S. (2005) "Russia: Kyrgyzstan's Friend in Need?" Eurasia Insight, 26/01/2005: http://courses.wcupa.edu/rbove/eco343/050Compecon/Soviet/Kyrgyz/050126russia.txt, retrieved 30/03/2015.

Blank, S. (1995) "Energy, Economics and Security in Central Asia: Russia and its Rivals," Strategic Studies Institute, U.S. Army War College,

Carlisle: http://www.strategicstudiesinstitute.army.mil/pubs/download.cfm?q=119, retrieved 23/01/2016.

Bogatyrev, B. (2007) "Osobennosti sovremennogo transita i problem identichnosti," [Particularities of modern transition and problems of identity] in: "Lapins, W. (2007) Istoriya I identichnost': Kyrgyzskaya Respublika/Geschichte und Idenität: Kirgisische Republik (text in Russian and German) *[History and Identity: The Kyrgyz Republic]*, Friedrich-Ebert-Foundation.

Bohr, A. (1998) "The Central Asian states as nationalizing regimes," In *Nation-Building in the Post-Soviet Borderlands: The Politics of National Identities*, edited by G. Smith, V. Law, A. Wilson, A. Bohr and E. Allworth. Cambridge: Cambridge University Press.

Bohr, A. (2010) "Revolution in Kyrgyzstan – Again," *Russia and Eurasia Programme Paper* 03/10, Chatham House: https://www.chathamhouse.org/sites/files/chathamhouse/public/Research/Russia%20and%20Eurasia/0410pp_kyrgyzstan.pdf, retrieved 31/03/2015.

Bond, A. & Koch, N. (2010) "Interethnic Tensions in Kyrgyzstan: A political geographic perspective," in: *Eurasian Geography and Economics*, 51.4, 531–562.

Brown, D. (1999) "Are there Good and Bad Nationalisms?." *Nations and Nationalism* 5.2, 281–302.

Brubaker, R. (1996) *Nationalism Reframed: Nationhood and the National Question in the New Europe*. Cambridge: Cambridge University Press.

Brubaker, R. (2000) "Accidental Diasporas and 'External Homelands' in Central and Eastern Europe: Past and Present," *Reihe Politikwissenschaft* 71, Institute for Advanced Studies, University of Vienna.

Brzezinski, Z. (1999) *Velikaia shakhmatnaia doska*, Moskva: Mezhdunarodnye otnosheniia.

Bugubaev, K. (2013) "Kyrgyzstan-Russia Relations," in: *Strategic Outlook*: http://strategicoutlook.org/publications/Kyrgyzstan_Russia_Relations.pdf, retrieved 04/03/2015.

Bukh, A. (2010) *Japan's national identity and foreign policy: Russia as Japan's "other,"* Abingdon, Oxon: Routledge.

Burke, P. (2000) "Identity Theory and Social Identity Theory," *Social Psychology Quarterly* 63, 224–37.

Burke, P. & Stets, J. (2009) *Identity Theory*, Oxford: Oxford University Press.

Carrère d'Encausse, H. (1979) *Decline of an Empire: The Soviet Socialist Republics in Revolt*, New York: Newsweek Books.

Carrère d'Encausse, H. (1993) *The End of the Soviet Empire. The Triumph of Nations*, New York: Basic Books.

Chatham House (2013) "Eurasian Economic Integration: Rhetoric and Reality," *Russia and Eurasia Summary*: http://www.chathamhouse.org/sites/files/chathamhouse/public/Research/Russia%20and%20Eurasia/180713summary.pdf, retrieved 22.02.2015.

Chatterjee, S. (2003) "Neo-realism, Neo-liberalism and Security," *International Studies* 40.2, 125–144.

Chernov, V. (2009) "Organizatsiia Dogovora o Kollektivnoi Bezopasnosti Kak Institut Mezhgosudarstvennoi Voenno-Politicheskoi Integracii Na Postsovetskom Postranstve," [The CSTO as the Institute of Inter-State Military and Political Integration on the Post-Soviet Space], Phd dissertation, Kyrgyz-Russian-Slavonic University: Bishkek: oel.bik.org.kg/ru/download/608/, retrieved 21/03/2015.

Cholponkulova, A. (2000) *Kontitutsionnye Osnovi Bneshnepoliticheskoi Deyatl'nosti Kyrgyzskoi Republiki [The constitutional basis of Foreign Policy Activities of the Kyrgyz Republic]*, Bishkek: Biyiktik.

Clunan, A. (2009) *The social construction of Russia's resurgence: aspirations, identity, and security interests*, Baltimore: John Hopkins University.

Cohen, R. (2001) *Global diasporas: an introduction*, London: Routledge.

Collins, K. (1999) "Clans, Pacts, and Politics: Understanding Regime Transition in Central Asia," *Journal of Democracy* 13.3, 137–152.

Collins, K. (2004) "The Logic of Clan Politics: Evidence from the Central Asian Trajectories," *World Politics*, 56.2, 24–61.

Collins, K. (2006) *Clan Politics and Regime Transformation in Central Asia*, New York: Cambridge University Press.

Collins, K. (2011) "Kyrgyzstan's Latest Revolution," *Journal of Democracy* 22.3, 150–164, Johns Hopkins University Press.

Cummings, S. (2003) "Eurasian bridge or murky waters between east and west? Ideas, Identity and output in Kazakhstan's foreign policy," *Journal of Communist Studies and Transition Politics* 19.3, 139–155.

Cummings, S. (2013) "Leaving Lenin: elites, official ideology and monuments in the Kyrgyz Republic," *Nationalities Papers: The Journal of Nationalism and Ethnicity*, 41.4, 606–621.

Cummings, S. & Ryabkov, M. (2008) "Situating the 'Tulip Revolution'," *Central Asia Survey* 27.3–4, 241–252.

Cummings, S. (2013) *Symbolism and Power in Central Asia: Politics of the Spectacular*, London: Routledge.

Cummings, S., Juraev, Sh., Pugachev, A., Temirkulov, A., Tiulegenov, M., Tursunkulova, B. (2013) "State, regime, and government in the Kyrgyz Republic (1991–2010): disaggregating a relationship," in: *East European Politics*, 29.4, 443–460.

Dagiev, D. (2013) *Regime Transition in Central Asia: Stateness, Nationalism and Political Change in Tajikistan and Uzbekistan*, London: Routledge.

Demo, D. (1992) "The Self-Concept Over Time: Research Issues and Directions," *Annual Review of Sociology* 181.1, 303–326.

Development Policy Institute Bishkek (DPI), "Materialy obshchestvennogo obsuzhdenia "Bezrabotitsa v Kyrgyzskoi Respublike: ugrozy i puti ikh preodolenia" in *Bezraboitsa—Eto Simptom Bolezni Pod Nazvaniem 'Slabost' Mestnogo Samoupravleniia*, 18/04/2011: www.dpi.kg/ru/news/full/239.htm, retrieved 21/012015.

Deyermond, R. (2009) "Matrioshka hegemony: multi-levelled hegemonic competition and security in post-Soviet Central Asia," *Review of International Studies*, 35, 151–173.

DeYoung, A. (2006) "Problems and trends in education in Central Asia since 1990: the case of general secondary education in Kyrgyzstan," *Central Asian Survey* 25.4, 499–514.

Digol, D. (2012) "Russia's foreign policy in Central Asia: From Yeltsin to Medvedev," in Freire, M., and Kanet, R., *Russia and its Near Neighbours*, London: Palgrave, 174–200.

Domashev, N. (2010) "Limits to Kinship Politics in Kyrgyzstan," Master Thesis: Central European University, Budapest: http://www.etd.ceu.hu/2010/domashev_nikolay.pdf, retrieved 19/04/2015.

Elebaeva, A. & Omuraliev, N. (1998) "Mezhetnicheskie otnosheniia v Kyrgyzstane: Dinamika i tendentsii razvitiia" *[Interethnic Relations in Kyrgyzstan: Dynamics and Tendencies of Development]*, CA&CC Press, Sweden: http://www.ca-c.org/journal/15-1998/st_07_elebaeva.shtml, retrieved 01/03/2015.

Engvall, J. (2011) "Flirting with State Failure. Power and Politics in Kyrgyzstan since Independence," *Silk Road Paper*, Central Asia - Caucasus

Institute & Silk Road Studies Program – A Joint Transatlantic Research and Policy Center, Washington/Stockholm.

Engvall, J. & Laruelle, M. (2015) *Kyrgyzstan beyond "Democracy Island" and "Failing State:" Social and Political Changes in a Post-Soviet Society*, London: Lexington Books.

Eshimkanov, M. et al. (1995) *A. Akaev: Pervii President Nezavisimogo Kyrgyzstana [A. Akaev: The First President of Independent Kyrgyzstan]*, Bishkek: Asaba.

Everett-Heath, T. (2003) *Central Asia: Aspects of Transition*, London: Routledge.

Fairclough, N. (1995) *Critical Discourse Analysis*, London: Longman.

Fawn, R. (2003) *Ideology and national identity in post-communist foreign policies*, London: Frank Cass.

Finnemore, M. (1996) *National interests in international society*, London: Cornell University Press.

Finnemore, M. (1996b) "Norms, Culture and World Politics: insights from sociology's institutionalism," *International Organization*, 1996, 50.2, pp. 325–347.

Fumagalli, M. (2007a) "Ethnicity, state formation and foreign policy: Uzbekistan and 'Uzbeks abroad'," *Central Asian Survey* 26.1, 105–122.

Fumagalli, M. (2007b) "Framing ethnic minority mobilization in Central Asia: The cases of Uzbeks in Kyrgyzstan and Tajikistan," in: *Europe-Asia Studies*, 59.4, 567–590.

Gellner, E. (1983) *Nations and Nationalism*, Oxford: Blackwell.

Gleason, G. (1997) *The Central Asian States: Discovering Independence*, Boulder, CO: Westview Press.

Gleason, G. (2001) "Foreign policy and domestic reform in Central Asia," *Central Asian Survey*, 20.2, 167–182.

Goehring, J. & Walker, C. (2008) "Petro-authoritarianism and Eurasia's New Divides," in *Nations in Transit 2008*, Freedom House: https://freedomhouse.org/report/nations-transit-2008/essay-petro-authoritarianism-and-eurasias-new-divides#.VME8-1pOhls, retrieved 22/01/2015.

Gross, J. (1992) *Muslims in Central Asia: Expressions of Identity and Change*, Durham, N.C.: Duke University Press.

Gumppenberg, M.-C. von (2002) *Staats- und Nationsbildung in Kazachstan*; Opladen: Leske + Budrich.

Hale, H. (2005) "Regime cycles: democracy, autocracy, and revolution in Post-Soviet Eurasia," *World Politics* 58.1, 133–165.

Hanks, R. (2011) "Crisis in Kyrgyzstan: conundrums of ethnic conflict, national identity and state cohesion," *Journal of Balkan and Near Eastern Studies* 13.2, 177–187.

Hauner, M. (2013) *Russia's Asian Heartland Yesterday and Today*, London: Routledge.

Hirschman, A. (1970) *Exit, voice and loyalty: responses to decline in firms, organizations, and states*, Cambridge, Mass.: Harvard University Press.

Hobsbawm, E. (1991) *Nations and Nationalism Since 1780: Programme, Myth, Reality*, Cambridge: Cambridge University Press.

Hopf, T. (2002) *Social construction of international politics: identities & foreign policies, Moscow 1955 and 1999*, London: Cornell University Press.

Hopf, T. (1998) "The Promise of Constructivism in International Relations Theory. *International Security* 22.1, 171–200.

Horton, A. & Brashinsky, M. (1992): *The zero hour: glasnost and Soviet cinema in transition*, Pricenton University Press, Princeton.

Hroch, M. (2007) *Comparative studies in modern European history: nation, nationalism and social change*, Aldertshot: Ashgate.

Huskey, E. (1993) "Akaev, Askar," in: Wieczynski, J. (ed.) *The Gorbachev Encyclopedia: Gorbachev: the Man and His Times*, Salt Lake City: Charles Schlacks, Jr., Publisher 31.

Huskey, E. (1993a) "Kyrgyzstan leaves the Ruble Zone," *RFE/RL Research Report* 35, 38–43.

Huskey, E. (1995) "The politics of language in Kyrgyzstan," *Nationalities Papers* 23.3, 549–572.

Huskey, E. (1997) "Kyrgyzstan: The fate of political liberalization," in Dawisha, K. & Parrott, B. *Conflict, Cleavage and Change in Central Asia and the Caucasus*, Cambridge: Cambridge University Press.

Huskey, E. (2006) "National identity from scratch: Defining Kyrgyzstan's role in world affairs," *Journal of Communist Studies and Transitional Politics*, 19.3, 111–138.

Huskey, E. (2008) "Foreign Policy in a Vulnerable State: Kyrgyzstan as Military Entrepot between the Great Powers," *Central Asia-Caucasus Institute & Silk Road Studies Program: China and Eurasia Forum Quarterly* 6.4, 5–18.

Ignatieff, M. (1993) *Blood and Belonging: Journeys into the New Nationalism*, New York: Farrar, Straus, Giroux.

International Crisis Group (ICG) (2010) "Kyrgyzstan: A Hollow Regime Collapses," *Asia Report 102*, Bishkek/Brussels, 27/04/2010: http://www.crisisgroup.org/~/media/Files/asia/centralasia/kyrgyzstan/B102%20Kyrgyzstan%20-%20A%20Hollow%20Regime%20Collapses.pdf, retrieved 21/03/2005.

International Crisis Group (ICG) (2012) "Kyrgyzstan: Widening Ethnic Divisions in the South," *Asia Report* 222, 29/03/2012: http://www.crisisgroup.org/en/regions/asia/central-asia/kyrgyzstan/222-kyrgyzstan-widening-ethnic-divisions-in-the-south.aspx, retrieved 10/04/2015.

Irving, L., Belanger, L., Ouellet, R., Curien, P. (2011) *Role theory in international relations: approaches and analysis*, London: Routledge.

Jackson, P. (2004) "Bridging the Gap: Toward A Realist-Constructivist Dialogue," *International Studies Review* 6, 337–352.

Jackson, N. (2010) "The role of external factors in advancing non-liberal democratic forms of political rule: a case study of Russia's influence on Central Asian regimes," *Contemporary Politics*, 16.1, 101–118.

Jackson, N. (2014) "The role of external factors in advancing non-liberal democratic forms of political rule: a case study of Russia's influence on Central Asian regimes," in: *International Politics and National Political Regimes: Promoting Democracy – Promoting Autocracy:* London: Routledge.

Johnson, L. (2004) *Vladimir Putin and Central Asia: The shaping of Russian foreign policy*, London: I.B. Tauris.

Jones Luong, P. (2002) *Institutional Change and political continuity in Post-Soviet Central Asia: power, perceptions, and pacts*, Cambridge: Cambridge University Press.

Jorgensen, M. & Phillips, L. (2002) *Discourse Analysis as Theory and Method*, Sage Publications: London.

Juraev, S. (2008) "Kyrgyz Democracy? The Tulip Revolution and Beyond," *Central Asian Survey*, 27, 253–264.

Kandiyoti, D. (1996) "Modernization without the Market? The Case of the 'Soviet East'," *Economy and Society*, 25, 4, pp. 529–542.

Kasenov, O. (1998) "Central Asia: national, regional and global aspects of security," in Allison, R., Bluth, C., Russia and Eurasia Program, *Security Dilemmas in Russia and Eurasia*, London: Royal Institute of International Affairs.

Katzenstein, P. (1996) *The Culture of National Security: Norms and Identity in the World Politics*, Columbia University Press: New York.

Katzenstein, P., Keohane, R. and Krasner, S. (1998) "International Organization and the Study of World Politics," *International Organisations*, 52, 645–85.

Khamidov, A. (2006) "Forging Broken Links. Uzbeks and the State in Kyrgyzstan. Institute for Public Policy," http://www.ipp.kg/ru/print/295/, retrieved 30/03/2015.

Khan, V. (2005) "On the Problem of Revival and Survival of Ethnic-Minorities in Post- Soviet Central Asia," in: Schlyter, B. (ed.) *Prospects for Democracy in Central Asia*, Swedish Research Institute in Istanbul.

Kleveman, L. (2003) *The New Great Game: Blood and Oil in Central Asia*, London: Atlantic Books.

Knyazev, A. (2008) "Etnicheskaia identichnost' i organizatsionnye problemy russkich i russkoiazychnych obshchin v Kirgizii i Centralnoi Azii" [Ethnic Identity and Organizational Problems of Russians and Russophone Communities in Kyrgyzstan and Central Asia], 28/02/2008: http://www.knyazev.org/stories/html/chang_290908.shtml, retrieved 22/03/2015.

Koichumanov, T., Otorbaev, J., Starr, F. (2005) "Kyrgyzstan: The Path Forward," *Central Asia Caucasus Institute: Silk Road Paper*.

Kolln, T. & Rohde, A. (2013) "The Uzbek Minority in Kyrgyzstan – Discrimination and Democracy," Master Thesis, Department for Society and Globalization, Roskilde University.

Kolstø, P. (2000) "Ethnicity and Subregional Relations: The Role of Russian Diasporas," in Dwan, R & Pavliuk, O. *Building Security in the New States of Eurasia: Subregional Cooperation in the Former Soviet Space*, 225, 38, Armonk, NY: M. E. Sharpe.

Kratochwil, F. (1989) *Rules, Norms and Decisions: on the conditions of practical and legal reasoning in international relations and domestic affairs*, Cambridge: Cambridge University Press.

Kulmatova, G. (2004) "Kyrgyzstan - Zapad: Novyi etap otnoshenii," [Kyrgyzstan - The West: A new level of relations], Yerevan: Russian-Armenian-University.

Landau, J. & Kellner-Heinkele, B. (2001) *Politics of language in the ex-Soviet Muslim states: Azerbayjan, Uzbekistan, Kazakhstan, Kyrgyzstan, Turkmenistan, Tajikistan*, London: Hurst and Company.

Landau, J. & Kellner-Heinkele, B. (2011) *Language Politics in Contemporary Central Asia: national and ethnic identity and the Soviet Legacy*, London: I.B. Tauris.

Lapid, Y. & Kratochwil, F. (eds.) (1996) *The Return of Culture and Identity in IR Theory*, Boulder: Lynne Riener.

Lapins, W. (2007) *Istoriia i identichnost': Kyrgyzskaia Respublika/Geschichte und Idenität: Kirgisische Republik* (text in Russian and German) *[History and Identity: The Kyrgyz Republic]*, Friedrich-Ebert-Foundation.

Laruelle, M. (2007) "Religious revival, nationalism and the 'invention of tradition': political Tengrism in Central Asia and Tatarstan," *Central Asian Survey* 26.2, 203–216.

Laruelle, M. (2012) "The paradigm of nationalism in Kyrgyzstan. Evolving narrative, the sovereignty issue, and political agenda," *Communist and Post-Communist Studies* 45, 39–49.

Lewis, D. (2008) "The Dynamics of Regime Change: Domestic and International Factors in the 'Tulip Revolution'," *Central Asian Survey*, 27, 265–277.

Linn, J. (2004) "Economic (Dis)Integration Matters: The Soviet Collapse Revisited," Paper prepared for a conference on "Transition in the CIS: Achievements and Challenges" at the Academy for National Economy, Moscow, September 13–14, 2004: http://www.brookings.edu/~/media/research/files/papers/2004/10/russia%20linn/200410linn.pdf, retrieved 18/04/2015.

Lubin, N. (1999) "New Threats in Central Asia and the Caucasus: An Old Story with a New Twist," in Menon, R., Federov, Y., Nodia, G. Russia, *The Caucasus and Central Asia: The 21st Century Security Environment*, New York: M.E. Sharpe.

Macedo, J. (2010): "What is driving the US, Russia and China in Central Asia's New- Great Game?" University of Dundee: Scotland:

http://www.dundee.ac.uk/cepmlp/gateway/files.php?file=cepmlp_car14_61_707592600.pdf, retrieved 20/04/2015.

Mahoney, J. (2000) "Path Dependence in Historical Sociology," *Theory and Society* 29.4, 507–548.

Malaschenko, A. (2013) *The Fight for Influence: Russia in Central Asia*, United Book Press: Carnegie Endowment for International Peace, Washington.

Marat, E. (2006) "Kyrgyz government unable to produce new national ideology," *Central Asia-Caucasus Institute Analyst* 8.4, 3–4.

Marat, E. (2007) "State-Propagated Narratives about a National Defender in Central Asian States," *The Journal of Power Institutions in Post-Soviet Societies* 6.7: http://pipss.revues.org/545, retrieved 13/05/2014.

Marat, E. (2008a) "Imagined Past, Uncertain Future: The Creation of National Ideologies in Kyrgyzstan and Tajikistan," in: *Problems of Post-Communism*, 55, 12–24.

Marat, E. (2008b) "National Ideology and State-Building in Kyrgyzstan and Tajikistan," Washington D.C.: *Central Asia-Caucasus Institute, John Hopkins University*; Uppsala: Silk Road Studies Program.

Marat, E. (2011) "Kyrgyzstan's Chaotic Foreign Policy," *Eurasia Daily Monitor* 8.121, 23/06/2011, 13:31: http://www.jamestown.org/single/?no_cache=1&tx_ttnews%5Btt_news%5D=38087#.VRr7TrqDpls, retrieved 31/03/2015.

Marx, K. (1954) "The eighteenth Brumaire of Louis Bonaparte," 3rd. rev. ed., Lawrence & Wishart.

Matveeva, A. (2007) "Russia's Policy in Central Asia," *International Spectator* 42.1.

Matveeva, A. (2009) "Legitimizing Central Asian Authoritarianism: Political Manipulation and Symbolic Power," *Europe-Asia Studies* 61.7, 1095–1121.

Matveeva, A. (2011) "Violence in Kyrgyzstan, Vacuum in the Region. The case for Russia-EU Joint Crisis Management," *LSE Civil Society & Human Security Research Unit Working Paper* 02.11: http://www.lse.ac.uk/internationalDevelopment/research/CSHS/pdfs/workingPapers/violenceInKyrgystan.pdf, retrieved 10/04/2015.

Matveeva, A. (2013) "Russia's changing security role in Central Asia," *European Security*, 22.4, 478–499.

McFaul, M. (2005) "Transitions from post-Communism," *Journal of Democracy* 16.3, 5–19.

McGlinchey, E. (2003) "Paying for Patronage: Regime Change in Post-Soviet Central Asia," Doctoral Dissertation, Princeton University.

Mearsheimer, J. (2001) *The Tragedy of Great Power Politics*, London: Norton.

Megoran, N. (2002) "The Borders of Eternal Friendship? The politics and pain of nationalism and identity along the Uzbekistan-Kyrgyzstan Ferghana Valley boundary, 1999–2000," Ph.D dissertation, Sidney Sussex College, Cambridge.

Megoran, N. (2012) "Averting Violence in Kyrgyzstan: Understanding and Responding to Nationalism," *Russia and Eurasia Programme Paper* 2012/03, Chatham House: London.

Moller, J. (2007) "The post-communist tripartition, 1996–2004," Contrasting actor- centered and structural explanations of political change in post-communist setting, EUI Working Papers, Badia Fiesolana, Italy: European University Institute.

Mullerson, R. (2009) *Central Asia: A Chessboard and Player in the New Great Game*, Abingdon: Routledge.

Murzakulova, A. & Schoeberlein, J. (2009) "The Invention of Legitimacy: Struggles in Kyrgyzstan to Craft an Effective Nation-State Ideology," *Europe-Asia Studies* 61.7, 1229–1248.

Murzakulova, A. & Dyatlenko, P. (2012) "Politika upravleniia etnokul'turnym mnogoobraziem v Kyrgyzstane: proshloe, nastoiashee, budushchee?" [Politics of administrating ethno-cultural diversity in Kyrgyzstan: past, present, future?], *Center "Polis" Asia*, Bishkek: http://soros.kg/wp-content/uploads/2012/02/analiticalreport_policeasia1.pdf, retrieved 01/03/2015.

Nagatomo, Y. (2011) "De-Territorialized Ethnic Community: The Residential Choices and Networks among Japanese Lifestyle Migrants in South East Queensland," *Japanese Studies* 31.3, 423–440.

Nichol, J. (2005) "Coup in Kyrgyzstan: Development and Implications," *Congressional Research Service: Report for Congress*, 14/04/2005: http://fas.org/sgp/crs/row/RL32864.pdf, retrieved 21/03/2015.

Nichol, J. (2010) "The April 2010 Coup in Kyrgyzstan and its Aftermath: Context and Implications for U.S. Interests," *Congressional Research*

Service: Report for Congress, 15/06/2010: http://fas.org/sgp/crs/row/R41178.pdf, retrieved 10/04/2015.

Nixey, J. (2012) "The long goodbye: waning Russian influence in the South Caucasus and Central Asia," London: Briefing Paper, Chatham House, RIIA: http://www.chathamhouse.org/publications/papers/view/184065, retrieved 23.01.2015.

Ogden, C. (2008) "Diaspora Meets IR's Constructivism: An Appraisal," *Politics* 28.1, 1–10.

Olcott, M. (1995) "Sovereignty and the 'Near Abroad'," *Olbris* 39.3, 353–367.

Olcott, M. (1996a) *Central Asia's New States: Independence, Foreign Policy, and Regional Security*, Endowment of the United States Institute of Peace.

Olcott, M. (1996b) "Kyrgyzstan and the Kyrgyz," in: Smith, G. (ed.), *The Nationalities Question in the Post-Soviet States*, Longman: London & New York.

Olcott, M. (2011) "The 'Stans" in 20," Op-Ed, Real Instituto Elcano: http://carnegieeurope.eu/publications/?fa=46397, retrieved 24/01/2016.

Omarov, N. (2005) "Kyrgyzstan: v poiskakh priemlemoi al'ternativi," [Kyrgyzstan: in search of an acceptable alternative] *APN.kz* 26/12/2005: http://www.apn.kz/publications/article125.htm, retrieved 20/05/2015.

Omarov, N. (2011) "Kyrgyzskaya respublika. Iskhodnye uslovia transformatsii," [The Kyrgyz Republic: initial conditions of transformation] in *Politicheskii protsess v Tsentral'noi Azii: Rezul'tat, Problem, Perspektivi*, Moskva: IVRAN, TSSPI.

Omuralieva, M. (2008) "Kyrgyz Leadership and Ethnopolitics before and after the Tulip Revolution: The Changed Position of Ethnic Russians and Uzbeks," Master thesis, Central European University, Hungary: http://www.etd.ceu.hu/2008/omuralieva_munara.pdf, retrieved 19/04/2015.

Ong, A. (1998) *Flexible Citizenship: The Cultural Logic of Transnationality*, London: Duke University Press.

Orlov, D. (2009) "V chem tragediia 'Russkoi Kirgizii," [On the tragedy of the "Russian Kyrgyzstan"] *Russkii Dom* 04/01/2009: http://www.russdom.ru/node/922, retrieved 16/04/2015.

Ortmann, S. (2010) "Diffusion as discourse of danger: Russian self-representations and the framing of the Tulip Revolution," *Central Asian Survey* 27.3–4, 367–378.

Oruzbaev, A. (ed.) (2003) *Russkii iazyk v Kyrgyzstane [Russian Language in Kyrgyzstan]*, Bishkek: Kyrgyz-Russian Slavonic University.

Oruzbaev, A. et al. (2008) "Multilingualism, Russian language and education in Kyrgyzstan," *International Journal of Bilingual Education and Bilingualism* 11/3–4, 476–500.

Paasi, A. (1996) "Inclusion, Exclusion and Territorial Identities," *Nordisk Samhallsgeografik Tidskrift* 23.

Paramonov, V., Strokov, A, Stolpovski, O. (2009) *Russia in Central Asia: Policy, Security and Economics*, Hauppauge New York: Nova Science Publishers.

Pastor, G. & Damjanovic, T. (2001) "The Russian financial crisis and its consequences for Central Asia," IMF Working Paper 1.169: https://www.imf.org/external/pubs/ft/wp/2001/wp01169.pdf, retrieved 10/03/2015.

Popescu, N. (2006) "Russia's Soft Power Ambitions," *Centre for European Policy Studies Policy Brief* no. 115, October (Brussels, CEPS): http://aei.pitt.edu/11715/1/1388.pdf, retrieved 17/04/2015.

Prizel, I. (1998) *National identity and foreign policy: nationalism and leadership in Poland, Russia and Ukraine*, Cambridge: Cambridge University Press.

Radnitz, S. (2006) "What really happened in Kyrgyzstan?" *Journal of Democracy*, 17.2, 132–146.

Ramphal, S. (1984) "Small is Beautiful but Vulnerable," *The Round Table* 292, 367–371.

Rashid, A. (1994) *The resurgence of Central Asia: Islam or Nationalism?*, Karachi: Oxford University Press.

Reinke de Buitrago, S. (2012) *Portraying the Other in International Relations: Cases of Othering, Their Dynamics and The Potential for Transformation*, Newcastle: Cambridge Scholars Publishing.

Robbins, B. (1998), "Introduction Part I: Actually Existing Cosmopolitanism" in P. Cheah and B. Robbins (eds.), *Cosmopolitics: Thinking and Feeling Beyond the Nation*, Minneapolis: University of Minnesota Press, pp. 1–19.

Rotar, I. (2006) "Uzbeks appeal to Bakiev, claiming ethnic discrimination," *Jamestown Foundation Eurasia Daily Monitor*, 3.29, 10/02/2006: http://www.jamestown.org/publications_details.php?volume_id.414&issue_id.3615&article_id=2370760, retrieved 21/03/2015.

Roy, O. (2000) *The New Central Asia: The Creation of Nations*, A. Danchev (ed.) Vol. 15, *The Library of International Relations*, London: I.B.Tauris.

Rudov, G. (2001) *Kyrgyzstan-Rossiia: istoriia vzaimootnoshenii suverennykh gosudarstv: 90-e gody XX veka) [Kyrgyzstan-Russia: a history of the interrelations of sovereign states: the 90s of the 20th century]*, Moscow/Bishkek: Ilim.

Ruget, V. & Usmanalieva, B. (2007) "The impact of state weakness on citizenship - a case study of Kyrgyzstan," in: *Communist and Post-Communist Studies* 40, 441–458.

Ryabkov, M. (2008) "The North-South Cleavage and Political Support in Kyrgyzstan," *Central Asian Survey*, 27.3–4, 301–316.

Saivetz, C. & Jones, A. (1994) *In Search of Pluralism: Soviet and Post-Soviet Politics*, Colorado: Westview Press.

Sakwa, R. (2007) *Putin: Russia's Choice*, 2nd ed. London: Routledge.

Sari, Y. (2012) "Foreign Policy of Kyrgyzstan under Askar Akayev and Kurmanbek Bakiyev," *PERCEPTIONS* XVII.3, 131–150.

Sergunin, A. & Karabeshkin, L. (2015) "Understanding Russia's Soft-Power Strategy," *Politics*, 35: 347–363.

Sewell, W. (1996) "Historical Events as Transformations of Structures: Inventing Revolution at the Bastille," *Theory and Society* 25.6, 841–81.

Shain, Y. & Barth, A. (2003) "Diasporas and International Relations Theory," *International Organization* 57.3, 449–480.

Shain, Y. (2007) *Kinship & Diasporas in International Affairs*, Ann Arbor: University of Michigan Press.

Shamkhal, A. (2012) "The 'New Great Game' over the Caspian Region: Russia, the USA, and China in the Same Melting Pot," *Khazar Journal of Humanities and Social Sciences* 15.2, 29–60.

Shulman, S. (2010) "Sources of Civic and Ethnic Nationalism in Ukraine," *Journal of Communist Studies and Transition Politics*, 18.4, 1–30.

Smith, A. (1991) *National Identity*, Reno, NV: University of Nevada Press.

Smith, A. (1996) "Culture, Community and Territory: The Politics of Ethnicity and Nationalism," *International Affairs*, 72.3, 445–458.

Smith, G. (1996) *The nationalities question in the post-Soviet states*, London: Longman.

Smith, G. (1999) "Transnational politics and the politics of the Russian diaspora," *Ethnic and Racial Studies* 22.3, 500–523.

Smith, G., Law, V., Wilson, A., Bohr, A. and Allworth, E. (1998) *Nation-building in the Post-Soviet Borderlands*, Cambridge: Cambridge University Press.

Spinner-Halev, J. & Theiss-Morse, E. (2003) "National Identity and Self Esteem," *Perspectives on Politics* 1.3, pp. 515–532.

Spector, R. (2004) "The Transformation of Askar Akaev, President of Kyrgyzstan," Berkeley: *Program in Soviet and Post-Soviet Studies Working Paper Series*: http://iseees.berkeley.edu/bps/publications/2004_02-spec.pdf, retrieved 01/03/2015.

Suny, R. (1999) "Southern Tears: Dangerous Opportunities in the Caucasus and Central Asia," in: Menon, R., Federov, Y., Nodia, G. Russia, *The Caucasus and Central Asia: The 21st Century Security Environment*, New York: M.E. Sharpe.

Suny, R. G. (2000) "Provisional stabilities: the politics of identities in post-Soviet Eurasia," *International Security* 24.3, 139–178.

Suny, R. G. (2001) "Constructing primordialism: old histories for new nations," *The Journal of Modern History* 73, 862–896.

Tajfel, H. (1978) *Differentiation between social groups: studies in the social psychology of intergroup relations*, London/ New York: Published in cooperation with European Association of Experimental Social Psychology by Academic Press.

Tchoroev, T. (2002) "Historiography of post-Soviet Kyrgyzstan," *International Journal of Middle East Studies* 34, 351–374.

Temirkulov, A. (2010) "Kyrgyz 'revolutions' in 2005 and 2010: comparative analysis of mass mobilization," *Nationalities Papers* 38.5, 589–600.

Trenin, D. (2007) "Russian and Central Asia," in: Rumer, E., Trenin, D., Huasheng, Z. (2007) *Central Asia. Views from Washington, Moscow and Beijing*, New York: ME. Sharpe.

Troitskiy, E. (2011) "Political Turbulence in Kyrgyzstan and Russian Foreign Policy," *Uibrief* 10, Stockholm: The Swedish Institute of International Affairs.

Tromble, R. (2014) "Securitizing Islam, Securitizing Ethnicity: the dismal of Uzbek radicalism in Kyrgyzstan," *East European Politics* 30.4, 526–547.

Tufaro, E. (2014) "Fatal attraction? Russia's soft power in its neighborhood – Analysis," Eurasiareview: http://fride.org/download/29.05.2014_EurasiaReview_US_ET.pdf, retrieved 11/04/2015.

Turner, V. (1967) "Betwixt and Between: The Liminal Period in Rites de Passage," in Turner, V. *The Forest of Symbols*, Ithaca: Cornell University Press.

Turner, R. (1968) "The self-conception in social interaction" in: Gordon & Gergen (ed.), *The New Self in Social Interaction*, Vol. 1, 299–308.

Umland, A. (2012) "Russia's Speading Nationalist Infection," *Foreign Policy Journal*, 18/04/2012: http://www.foreignpolicyjournal.com/2012/04/18/russias-spreading-nationalist-infection/, retrieved 07/02/2016.

Vachudova, M. (2005) *Europe undivided*, Oxford: Oxford University Press.

van Schendel, W. & Zürcher, E. (2001) *Identity Politics in Central Asia and the Muslim World: nationalism, ethnicity and labour in the twentieth century*, London: I.B. Tauris.

Wachtel, A. B. (2013) "Kyrgyzstan between democratization and ethnic intolerance," *Nationalities Papers* 41.6, 971–986.

Walker, R.B.J. (2002) "On the Immanence/Imminence of Empire," *Millennium: Journal of International Studies* 31.2, 337–345.

Wendt, A. (1999) *Social theory of international politics*, Cambridge: Cambridge University Press.

Wood, T. (2006) "Kyrgyzstan's Place in the World," Conference Paper presented at TOSCCA Workshop: Kyrgyzstan at the Cross-Roads, Oxford.

Wu, Y. (2011) "Russia and the CIS in 2010," in *Asian Survey*, 51.1, 64–75.

Zevelev, I. (2008) "Russia's Policy Toward Compatriots in the Former Soviet Union," *Russia in Globe Affairs*, 1.1: http://eng.globalaffairs.ru/number/n_10351, retrieved 22.01.2015.

Ziegler, C. (2006) "The Russian Diaspora in Central Asia: Russian Compatriots and Moscow's Foreign Policy," in: *Demokratizatsiia: The Journal of Post-Soviet Democratization* 14.1, 103–126.

Speeches, Laws, Decrees, National Programs, Reports, Statistics and Official Statements from the Russian Federation, the Kyrgyz Republic and International Organizations

Human Rights Watch (HRW)

World Report 2014: Kyrgyzstan (Events of 2013): https://www.hrw.org/world-report/2014/country-chapters/kyrgyzstan, retrieved 08/02/2016.

National Democratic Institute (NDI)

Statement of the National Democratic Institute (NDI) International Election Observer Delegation to Kyrgyzstan's October 29, 2000 Presidential Election. Bishkek, October 31, 2000: https://www.ndi.org/files/kg_electobs.pdf, retrieved 12/03/2016.

Organization for Security and Cooperation in Europe/Office for Democratic Institutions and Human Rights (OSCE/ODIHR)

Kyrgyz Republic – Presidential Elections, 29 October 2000, ODIHR Final Report: http://www.osce.org/odihr/elections/kyrgyzstan/15802?download=true, retrieved 28/01/2016.

The Russian Federation

MID Rossiiskoi Federatsii – Ministry of Foreign Affairs of the Russian Federation Rezoluciia chetvertogo kongressa sootechestvennikov, prozhivaiushich za rubezhom, 28/10/2012: http://www.mid.ru/brp_4.nsf/newsline/CEFF12BB3206904A44257AAA004381D5 retreived 22/01/2015.

The Kyrgyz Republic

Results of the first census conducted in the Kyrgyz Republic in 1999 (incl. 1959–1989): http://www.stat.kg/stat.files/census.pdf, retrieved 03/05/14.

Results of the second census conducted in the Kyrgyz Republic in 2009: http://www.waikato.ac.nz/__data/assets/pdf_file/0004/180544/Kyrgyzstan-2009-en.pdf, retrieved 04/04/15.

Postanovlenie Kabineta Ministrov Respubliki Kyrgyzstan, No. 18, "O respublikanskom biudzhete Respubliki Kyrgyzstan na 1992 god," [Decree

109

of the Ministerial Cabinet of the Republic of Kyrgyzstan, No. 18, "On the republican budget of the Republic of Kyrgyzstan for the year 1992], Bishkek, 17 January 1992: http://cbd.minjust.gov.kg/act/view/ru-ru/40345?cl=ru-ru, retrieved 06/03/2015.

Constitution of the Kyrgyz Republic of May 5, 1993, available in Russian at: http://bishkekinfo.kg/news/504, retrieved 07/03/2015.

Akaev, A. (1999) „Diplomatiia shelkovogo puti" [Diplomacy of the Silk Road: a foreign policy doctrine: the past and present of the great Silk Road], in: *Executive Intelligence Review* 26.15.

Kyrgyzstan – Rossija (90e gody XX veka): Sbornik Dokumentov i materialov, [Kyrgyzstan – Russia (the 90s of the 20th century): Collection of documents and materials], Bishkek, 2001.

Zakon Kyrgyzskoi Respubliki ob ofitsial'nom yazyke Kyrgyzskoi Respubliki ot 25.05.2005 [Law oft he Kyrgyz Republic on the official language of the Kyrgyz Republic of 25/05/2005], available at: http://russkg.ru/index.php?option=com_content&view=article&id=481:-q-q&catid=52:2010-12-19-09-41-19&Itemid=52, retrieved 09/03/2015.

Constitution of the Kyrgyz Republic of October 21, 2007, available in Russian at: http://www.base.spinform.ru/show_doc.fwx?regnom=223&oid n=_1Y2105UJV#_1Y2105UJV, retrieved 24/03/2015.

Constitution of the Kyrgyz Republic of June 27, 2010, available in Russian at: http://www.gov.kg/?page_id=263, retrieved 10/04/2015.

Ministerstvo Inostrannich Del: *Istoria Obrazovania Ministerstva Inostranniah Del Kirgizskoi Respublikii, Portal Gosudarstvennix Slujb* [The Ministry of Foreign Affairs: History of the formation of the Ministry of Foreign Affairs of the Kyrgyz Republic], available at: http://www.mfa.gov.kg/contents/view/id/27, retrieved 04/03/2015).

Speech by the President Roza Otunbaeva at the 20th anniversary of Kyrgyzstan's Independence Day 31/08/2011, Web Presence of the Embassy of the Kyrgyz Republic to the U.S.A. and Canada: http://www.kgembassy.org/index.php?option=com_content&view=article&id=133:speech-by-the-president-roza-otunbayeva-at-the-20th-anniversary-of-kyrgyzstans-independence-day&catid=1:latest-news&Itemid=237, retrieved 31/03/2015.

Kontseptsiia etnicheskoi politiki i konsolidatsii obshchestva Kyrgyzskoi Respubliki i plan deistvii do 2015 goda, ["Concept of Ethnic Policy and

Consolidation of the Society of the Kyrgyz Republic"], Bishkek 2011: http://www.president.kg/files/docs/kontseptsiya_ukrepleniya_edinstva_naroda_i_mejetnicheskih_otnosheniy_v_kr.pdf, retrieved 12/04/2015.

Kontseptsiia ukrepleniia edinstva naroda i mezhetnicheskich otnoshenii v Kyrgyzskoi Respublike [Concept on Strengthening National Unity and Interethnic Relations in the Kyrgyz Republic], Bishkek 2013: http://www.president.kg/files/docs/kontseptsiya_ukrepleniya_edinstva_naroda_i_mejetnicheskih_otnosheniy_v_kr.pdf, retrieved 12/04/2015.

The World Bank

Country Profile: Kyrgyz Republic: http://data.worldbank.org/country/kyrgyz-republic, retrieved 21/01/2015.

The World Bank: Migration and Remittance Flows in Europe and Central Asia: Recent Trends and Outlook, 2013–2016, 02/10/2013: http://www.worldbank.org/en/news/feature/2013/10/02/migration-and-remittance-flows-in-europe-and-central-asia-recent-trends-and-outlook-2013-2016, retrieved 17/04/2015.

UN Comtrade

Country Profile: Kyrgyzstan, last update 2012: http://comtrade.un.org/pb/CountryPagesNew.aspx?y=2013, retrieved 22.01.2014.

United Nations Statistics Division – Kyrgyzstan: http://unstats.un.org/unsd/snaama/resQuery.asp, retrieved 21/01/2015.

Online News Outlets and Collections

24Mir

"Putin: Rossijia prodolzhit gotovit' sotrudinikov dlia specsluzhb SNG," [Putin: Russia will continue to prepare the agents of secret services throughout the CIS], 10/07/2014, 14:15: http://mir24.tv/news/community/10856409, retrieved 21/01/2015.

24.kg

Gorbachev, I. (2007) "Partii 'Edinnaia Rossiia' i 'Sodruzhestvo' (Kyrgyzstan) podpisali dogovor o vzaimodeistvii i sotrudnichestve" [The Parties "Edinnaiya Rossiya" and "Sodruzhestvo" signed an agreement on interaction and cooperation], 02/10/2007, 17:56: http://arch.24.kg/politic/25110-2007/10/02/63869.html, retrieved 23/03/2015.

BBC Russian Service

"Medvedev prikazal zashchitit' rossian v Kirgizii," [Medvedev gave order to defend Russians in Kyrgyzstan], 20/04/2010, 17:46: http://www.bbc.co.uk/russian/international/2010/04/100420_belarus_bakiyev.shtml, retrieved 23/03/2015.

Bel'y Parus (paruskg.info)

"Kak 'Ar-Namys' za patriotism borolsia...pri izpolnenii gima Kyrgyzstana deputaty ZH-K zapreshaiut vsem grazhdanam nachodit'sya v golovnom ubore," ["How 'Ar-Namys' fought for patriotism ... members of parliament (ZH-K) prohibit the wearing of hats for all citizens of Kyrgyzstan when performing the national anthem], 25/02/2011, 15:55: http://www.paruskg.info/2011/02/25/40270, retrieved 10/04/2015.

Bishkek Press Club

Toralieva, G. (2008) "Razvitie SMI v Kyrgyzstane: Tendencii 2008 goda" [The Evolution of the Media Landscape in Kyrgyzstan: Tendencies in the year 2008], *Bishkek Press Club,* 17/09/2008: http://www.bpc.kg/perspective/forprint/94, retrieved 20/03/2015.

CA-News.info

"Kokoshin o puti resheniia krizisa v Kirgizii," [Kokoshin speaks about the path towards settlement of the crisis in Kyrgyzstan], 22/05/2005: https://ca-news.info/2005/03/22/44, retrieved 22/03/2015.

Centralasiaonline.com

Karimov, A. (2010) "New Kyrgyz party emphasizes co-operation among nationalities," 19/07/2010: http://centralasiaonline.com/en_GB/articles/caii/newsbriefs/2010/07/19/newsbrief-06, retrieved 26/03/2015.

Osmonaliev, O. (2013) "Kyrgyzstan aims for economic growth," 28/02/2013: http://centralasiaonline.com/en_GB/articles/caii/features/main/2013/02/28/feature-01, retrieved 22/01/2015.

CentrAzia – Centrasia.ru

Aiip, N. (2002) "Deputat A. Madumarov: Akaev narushil Konstituciiu podpisav sekretnii dogovor s Kitaem" [MP A. Madumarov: Akaev violated the constitution by signing a secret agreement with China], 20/05/2002, 09:27: http://www.centrasia.ru/newsA.php?st=1021872420, retrieved 01/02/2016.

Kozubekova, È. (2008) "NATO ili ODKB: Inogo ne dano dlia Kirgizii?" [NATO or CSTO: No other option for Kyrgyzstan?], 05/11/2008, 14:54: http://www.centrasia.ru/newsA.php?Month=11&Day=5&Year=2008, retrieved 26/03/2015.

Hoperskaya, L. (2010) "Nacionalizm v deistvii. Trevozhnie tendencii v Kirgizii," [Nationalism in action. Alarming tendencies in Kyrgyzstan], 15/04/2010: http://www.centrasia.ru/newsA.php?st=1271276400, retrieved 23/03/2015.

Nogoibaeva, È. (2010) "Formula Lassauèla dlia Kyrgyzstana, ili kak nas formatiruiut," [Lasswell's Formula applied to Kyrgyzstan, or how we are being formatted], 22/04/2010: http://www.centrasia.ru/newsA.php?st=1271880000, retrieved 22/03/2015.

CNN

Wedeman, B. (2010) "Kyrgyzstan's new leader tackled challenging job," 14/06/2010: http://edition.cnn.com/2010/WORLD/asiapcf/04/11/kyrgyzstan.otunbayeva/, retrieved 10/04/2015.

Current Digest of the Soviet Press

Vol. XLIII, no. 33, 1991. pp. 25n–26.

Diesel.elcat.kg

"Situaciia v Bishkeke 20 aprelia 2010 goda," [The Situation in Bishkek on April 20, 2010], 20/04/2010, 14:07: http://diesel.elcat.kg/lofiversion/index.php?t3810729-200.html, retrieved 23/03/2015.

Eurasianet.org

Trilling, D. & Deirdre, T. (2009) "Kyrgyzstan: President Bakiyev Wants to Close U.S. Military Base Outside Bishkek," 02/02/2009, 20:00: http://

www.eurasianet.org/departments/insightb/articles/eav020309b.shtml, retrieved 30/03/2015.

"Kyrgyzstan: Bakiyev stands up to Uzbekistan and Turkmenistan on hydropower projects," 06/05/2009, 20:00: http://www.eurasianet.org/departments/insightb/articles/eav050709d.shtml, retrieved 21/03/2015.

Trilling, D. & Umetov, C. (2010) "Kyrgyzstan: Is Putin Punishing Bakiyev?" 05/04/2010, 20:00: http://www.eurasianet.org/departments/insight/articles/eav040610a.shtml, retrieved 21/03/2015.

Trilling, D. (2010) "Kyrgyzstan: Russian press bashing Bakiyev," 29/03/2010, 19:00: http://www.eurasianet.org/departments/insightb/articles/eav033010.shtml, retrieved 22/01/2015.

Rickleton, C. (2013) "Kyrgyzstan: Bishkek's Hydropower Hopes Hinge on Putin's Commitment," 25/04/2013, 12:07: http://www.eurasianet.org/node/66883, retrieved 22.01.2015.

Kucera, J. (2012) "Bakiyev can be bought": U.S. Embassy Tied Rent for Kyrgyz Base to President's Reelection," 05/01/2012, 16:55: http://www.eurasianet.org/node/64797, retrieved 30/03/2015.

Kucera, J. (2012) "Russia, Manas and the CSTO: Q&A with Roza Otunbayeva," 14/12/2012, 12:50: http://www.eurasianet.org/node/66304, retrieved 31/03/2015.

Rickleton, C. (2013) "Kyrgyzstan: Nation-Building Efforts Reach the Silver Screen," 20/08/2013, 11:46: http://www.eurasianet.org/node/67411, retrieved 01/04/2015.

Fergananews.ru – International News Agency

"Shchas spoiu! Ili o tom, kak v parlamente Kirgizii podniali temu patriotizma," [I'm going to start singing! Or how the parliament of Kyrgyzstan raised the issue of patriotism] 30/09/2009: http://www.ferghana.ru/article.php?id.6314, retrieved 20/03/2015.

Kachiev, A. (2006) "Kyrgyzstan: Molodezh' Bishkeka aktivno protestuet protiv vstuplenie strany v HIPC" [Kyrgyzstan: Bishkek's youth is protesting actively against Kyrgyzstan's participation in the HIPC Dept initiative], 13/12/2006, 12:32: http://www.fergananews.com/articles/4780, retrieved 30/03/2015.

Ponomarev, V. (2007) "Alisher Saipov's assassination: Let's face the truth!" 10/12/2007, 15:51: http://enews.fergananews.com/articles/2262, retrieved 30/03/2015.

"V Moskve budet ustanovlen pamiatnik geroiu kyrgyzskogo eposa," [A monument will be dedicated to the hero of the Manas Epic in Moscow] 24/12/2006, 22:08: http://www.fergananews.com/news.php?id=4571, retrieved 24/03/2015.

Mamarianov, A. (2007) "Vybori v Krigizii: Administrativnii resurs i lichnosti kandidatov kak glavnie faktori pobedi," [Elections in Kyrgyzstan: Administrative resources and personalities as major determinants of victory] 14/12/2007, 18:12: http://www.fergananews.com/articles/5512, retrieved 25/03/2015.

Ivashenko, K. (2010) "Kamchibek Tashiev: Esli russkie, uzbeki ili turki skazhut, chto oni naravne s kyrgyzami ili vyshe ich, - gosudarstvo razvalitsya" [Kamchybek Tashiev: If Russians, Uzbeks or Turks said, that they are equal to or even superior to the Kyrgyz, the state would disintegrate], 16/09/2010, 17:53: http://www.fergananews.com/articles/6728, retrieved 10/04/2015.

"Kyrgyzstan: K. Tashiev priznal chto "Ata-Zhurt" – partiia nacionalistov, i rasskazal o pretentsiach k vremennomu pravitel'stvu [Kyrgyzstan: K.Tashiev admitted that "Ata Zhurt" is the party of nationalists, and spoke about the claims (his party holds) against the interim government], 28/01/2011, 13:55: http://www.fergananews.com/news.php?id=16292, retrieved 17/04/2015.

"Rossiya Podarila Pogranichnikam Kyrgyzstana Komplekt Voennoi Tekhniki na Summu v Polmilliarda Rubley," [Russia gave a set of military technology worth half a million rubles to Kyrgyzstan's border guards] 18/01/2012, 11:56: www.fergananews.com/news.php?id=17976, retrieved 22/01/2015.

Ivashchenko, E. (2012) OON: "Okolo Milliona Kyrgyzstantsev Krugly God Ispytyvaiut Nedostatok V Prodovol'stvii," [Approximately one million Kyrgyzstanis experience food shortages during the entire year] 31/01/2012, 15:20: www.fergananews.com/news.php?id=18060&mode=snews, retrieved 21/01/2015.

"President Kyrgyzstana A. Atambaev v Moskve: 'Manas – etnicheskii rossiyanin," [President of Kyrgyzstan A. Atambaev in Moscow: "Manas – an ethnic Russian] 24/02/2012, 17:23: http://www.fergananews.com/news.php?id=18236, retrieved 17/04/2015.

Forbes

Coyer, P. (2014) "Central Asia Stuck Between Sinking Russia and a Dominant China," 18/12/2014, 13:39: http://www.forbes.com/sites/paulcoyer/2014/12/18/pawns-no-more-central-asia-in-search-of-other-partners/, retrieved 17/04/2015.

Informacionno - Analiticheski Centr/ Center for Information and Analysis

Dyatlenko, P. (2008) "Iazykovaia Politika v Stranach Centralnoi Azii ostaetsia slozhnoi i protivorechivoi," [Language Policy in the states of Central Asia remains complicated and ambiguous] *Informacionno-analiticheskii centr*, 21/06/2008: http://www.ia-centr.ru/expert/1453/, retrieved 20/03/2015.

Institute for War and Peace Reporting (IWPR)

Amanov, T. (2006) "Kyrgyzstan: People's Assembly Disappoints," 12/08/06: https://iwpr.net/global-voices/kyrgyzstan-peoples-assembly-disappoints, retrieved 03/03/2015.

Mukhametrakhimova, S. (2011) "Kyrgyzstan Debates Rival Ethnic Policies," 01/06/2011: https://iwpr.net/global-voices/kyrgyzstan-debates-rival-ethnic-policies, retrieved 11/04/2015.

Dyatlenko, P. (2012) "Breakthrough for Outsider Party in Kyrgyzstan," 21/12/12: https://iwpr.net/global-voices/breakthrough-outsider-party-kyrgyzstan, retrieved 04/03/2015.

Kabar.kg

"Razrabatyvaetsia kontseptsiia etnicheskoi politiki i konsolidatsii obshchestva Kyrgyzstana," [A concept for nationalities policy and consolidation of society is in the making], 17/02/2011: http://www.kabar.kg/society/full/7269, retrieved 11/04/2015.

"'Jamestown:' Posle revolucii v Kyrgyzstane vneshniuiu politiku opredeliaiut vse, komu ne len'," [After the revolution, Kyrgyzstan's foreign policy is made by whoever feels like it] 24/06/2011: http://www.kabar.kg/rus/analytics/full/19186, retrieved 10/04/2015.

Komersant

"Protiv Rossii deistvuiut osoznanno i celenapravlenno, no na eto nel'zia obizhat'sia," [They act against Russia deliberately and determined, but one may not talk about it.] 07.04.2012, 13:24: http://kommersant.ru/doc/1911330, retrieved 22/01/2015.

Komsomol'skaya Pravda - Bishkek

"V Kyrgyzstane 23 sentiabria otnyne otmechaetsia kak den' gosudarstvennogo iazyka," [From now on, September 23 will be celebrated as the official day of the state language] 22/09/2009, 17:25: http://www.kp.kg/online/news/545306, retrieved 30/03/2015.

MSN – Online/MSN.kg

Coi, M. (2009) "Patriotism v defitsite," [A deficit of patriotism] 19/02/2009: http://www.msn.kg/ru/news/26656/, retrieved 20/03/2015.

Malevanaia, D. (2007) "Omut ideologii," [The slough of ideology] 31/07/2007: http://www.msn.kg/ru/news/19401/, retrieved 20/03/2015.

MID RF: "Russkie v Kirgisii podvergaiutsia napadeniam, vlasti ich ne zashishaiut," [Ministry of Interior of the Russian Federation: Russians in Kyrgyzstan are under attack, and the authorities are not defending them], 15/04/2010: http://www.newsru.com/russia/15apr2010/kyrgrus.html, retrieved 23/03/2015.

Nezavisimaja Gazeta

Panfilova, V. (2012) "Moskva dast Bishkeku shans," [Moscow gives Bishkek a chance] 20/02/2012, www.ng.ru/cis/2012-02-20/6_bishkek.html, retrieved 21/01/2014.

Politkom.ru

Hoperskaya, L. (2010) "Nacional-shovinizm po-kirgizki," [National-chauvinism the Kyrgyz way], 15/04/2010: http://politcom.ru/9954.html, retrieved 23/03/2015.

Pravda.ru

Balmasov, S. (2010) "Sud'ba russkich v Kirgizii: pogromy i perspektivy," [The fate of the Russians in Kyrgyzstan: pogroms and perspectives],

19/04/2010: http://www.pravda.ru/world/formerussr/other/19-04-2010/1028248-bishkek-0/, 23/03/2015.

Radio Free Europe/Radio Liberty (RFE/RL)

Djumataeva, V. (2010) "Moscow Chills Relations With Kyrgyzstan," 23/02/2010: http://www.rferl.org/content/Moscow_Chills_Relations_With_Kyrgyzstan/1966393.html, retrieved 21/03/2015.

Pannier, B. (2002) "Kyrgyzstan: In Annual Addresses, Kyrgyzstan's President Cites Foreign Policy Successes," (A summary of Akaev's 2002 Annual Address to the Parliament and the Nation), 17/10/2002: http://www.rferl.mobi/a/1101113.html, retrieved 10/03/2015.

"Kyrgyz Diplomats Obliged to Use Kyrgyz Language," 11/12/2009: http://www.rferl.org/content/Kyrgyz_Diplomats_Obliged_To_Use_Kyrgyz_Language_/1901817.html, retrieved 30/03/2015.

Blua, A. (2010) "Who is Roza Otunbaeva?," 08/04/2010: http://www.rferl.org/content/Who_Is_Roza_Otunbaeva/2006607.html, retrieved 17/04/2015.

Lagunina, I. (2011) "Doklady pravosashchitnych organizacii Mezhdunarodnaia amnictiia i Human Rights Watch [Reports of Human Rights Organizations Amnesty International and Human Rights Watch], 08/06/2011: http://www.svoboda.org/content/transcript/24229497.html, retrieved 07/02/2016.

"Priniata kontseptsiia etnicheskoi i politiki i konsolidatsii obshchestva" [A concept of ethnic policy and consolidation of society was passed], 18/06/2011: http://rus.azattyk.org/archive/ky_News_in_Russian_ru/20120724/4795/4795.html?id=24239070, retrieved 12/04/2015.

"Russia Smooths Ties With Kyrgyzstan," 06/04/2012: http://www.rferl.org/content/kyrgyzstan_russia_kant_manas_united_states_/24539255.html, retrieved 10/04/2015.

Pannier, B. (2014) "Who was Kurmanjan Datka and what does she mean to the Kyrgyz people?" 31/12/2014: http://www.rferl.org/content/qishloq-ovozi-who-was-kurmanjan-datka/26770979.html, retrieved 01/04/2015.

"Kyrgyz Abandon Uzbek for Secondary-School Graduation Test," 13/03/14: http://www.rferl.org/content/uzbekistan-kyrgyzstan-language-education-graduation/25296082.html, retrieved 08/02/2016.

Rambler.ru

"Referendum v Kyrgyzstane – poslednii shans dlia vosstanovleniia kirgizskoi gosudarstvennosti," [Referendum in Kyrgyzstan – Last chance for the establishment of Kyrgyz statehood] 29/06/2010, 09:22: http://news.rambler.ru/6819724/, retrieved 22/03/2015.

RBK

"D. Medvedev potreboval ot ministra oborony zashchitit' nachodiashchichsia v Kirgizii rossiian i ich sobstvennost," [D. Medvedev demanded from the Ministry of defense to protect lives and property of Russians currently residing in Kyrgyzstan], 20/04/2010, 18:39: http://www.ziwa.org/ru/Cluster.aspx?uid=2010042037&id=1-1&rid=-1&th=Медведев%2Вп отребовал%2Вминистра%2Вобороны, retrieved 23/03/2015.

Regnum – News Agency

"Èkspert: 'Kontseptsiia nacpolitiki partii 'Ata-Zhurt' traktuet natsiiu, kak v natsistskoi Germanii" [Expert: The concept of nationalities policy of the Ata-zhurt party treats the nationality like in Nazi Germany], 19/05/2011, 00:27: http://www.regnum.ru/news/polit/1406184.html, retrieved 11/04/2015.

Reuters

Fletcher, P. & Stamp, D. (2010) "Self-proclaimed Kyrygz leader thanks Russia," 08/04/2010, 12:40: http://www.reuters.com/article/2010/04/08/us-kyrgyzstan-unrest-russia-idUSTRE6373XN20100408, retrieved 10/04/2015.

RIA Novosti

"Kyrgyzstan Will Demand US Close the Base Eventually," 20/02/2008: http://en.rian.ru/world/20080220/99718840.html, retrieved 20/03/2015.

"SF razreshil FSB napravliat' sotrudnikov za granitsu na postoiannoi osnove," [Federal Council gave permission to the FSB to send agents on permanent basis abroad], 27/04/2013, 13:45: http://ria.ru/politics/20130427/934931983.html, retrieved 21/01/2015.

Rosbalt

Amelina, J. (2004) "Russkii jazyk v Kirgizii ostanetsia 'ofitsial'nym' na bumage." [The Russian language remains the "official" one in Kyrgyzstan. On paper], 13/03/2004, 13:23: http://www.rosbalt.ru/main/2004/03/13/149150.html, retrieved 05/03/2015.

Rossiiskaya Gazeta

Latukhina, K. "Troistvennyi vizit," [tripartite visit] 22/03/2012, 00:50: www.rg.ru/2012/03/21/putin.html, retrieved 22/05/2015.

RT News

"Kremlin will not intervene with military in Kyrgyzstan," 15/06/2010, 16:21: http://rt.com/news/kremlin-humanitarian-help-kyrgyzstan/, retrieved 21/01/2015.

Stoletie.ru

Shustov, A. (2010) "Russkie – uchodite!" [Russians – leave!], 16/04/2010: http://www.stoletie.ru/rossiya_i_mir/russkije--uhodite__2010-04-16.htm, retrieved 23/03/2015.

The Guardian

Ott, S. (2014) "Russia tightens control over Kyrgyzstan," 18/09/14, 17:00: http://www.theguardian.com/world/2014/sep/18/russia-tightens-control-over-kyrgyzstan, retrieved 22/01/2015.

The Journal of Turkish Weekly

Satke, R. (2011) "Kyrgyz" Project Remains Task Priority in Moscow," 07/07/2011: http://www.turkishweekly.net/op-ed/2845/kyrgyz-project-remains-task-priority-in-moscow.html, retrieved 31/03/2015.

The Moscow Times

Mereu, F. (2005) "Trading Hard Power for Soft Power," 24/03/2005, 00:00: http://www.themoscowtimes.com/news/article/trading-hard-power-for-soft-power/224340.html, retrieved 22.01.2015.

The New York Times

Kramer, A. E. (2010) "Uzbeks Accused of Inciting Violence in Kyrgyzstan," 02/07/2010: http://www.nytimes.com/2010/07/02/world/asia/02kyrgyzstan.html, retrieved 07/02/2016.

The Rural Development Fond (rdf.in.kg)

"Informaciya o 'DND Patriot'" [Information about 'DND Patriot'], 03/08/2010: http://www.rdf.in.kg/rus/dnd_patriot/, retrieved 10/04/2015.

The Times of Central Asia

"Kyrgyzstan won't compel its citizens to study Kyrgyz so far – Otunbayeva," 29/11/2011, 09:37: http://www.timesca.com/news/1369-kyrgyzstan-wont-compel-its-citizens-to-study-kyrgyz-so-far-otunbayeva, retrieved 31/03/2015.

Vechernii Bishkek

Coj, M. (2013) "Vneshnii dolg Kyrgyzstana sostavliaiet pochti polovinu VVP," 30/04/2013, 10:59: http://www.vb.kg/doc/226539_vneshniy_dolg_kyrgyzstana_sostavliaet_pochti_poloviny_vvp.html, retrieved 21/01/2015.

VOA News – Golos Ameriki/The Voice of America

"Roza Otunbaeva: Kyrgyzstan provodit mnogovektornuiu vneshnyuyu politiku," [Roza Otunbaeva: Kyrgyzstan pursues a multi-vector foreign policy] 15/06/2005, 00:00: http://m.golos-ameriki.ru/a/a-33-2005-06-15-voa2/602645.html, retrieved 21/03/2015.

Vremya Vostoka

Kerezovich, A. (2012): "Diasporal'noe povedenie russkich v Kyrgyzstane: optimisticheskii vzgliad" [Diasporal behavior of Russians in Kyrgyzstan: An optimist view], 27/07/2012, 16:24: http://easttime.ru/analytics/kyrgyzstan/diasporalnoe-povedenie-russkikh-v-kyrgyzstane-optimisticheskii-vzglyad, retrieved 23/03/2015.

"Rossiia gotovit kadry dlja bor'by s narkotikami v Kyrgyzstane," [Russia is preparing cadres to fight narcotics in Kyrgyzstan], 27/06/2013, 23:47: http://easttime.ru/news/kyrgyzstan/rossiya-gotovit-kadry-dlya-borby-s-narkotikami-v-kyrgyzstane/4243, retrieved 21/01/2015.

Vremya.ru
Dubnov, A. (2008) "Kto v Kirgizii choziain. U togo v rukach parlament" [Who is the master of the house in Kyrgyzstan? The one who controls the parliament.], 30/05/2008: http://www.vremya.ru/2008/94/5/204983.html, retrieved 30/03/2015.

Newspapers – Print editions

1. Delo N° (abb. DN)

Est. 1991 in Bishkek, Weekly Newspaper, Russian Language;
Chief editor: Svetlana Krasilnikova
Circulation: app. 30,000 in 1996, 16,000 in 2013;
Affiliation: pro-Russian, independent

The President of the Kyrgyz Republic (10/03/2004) "Ukaz Presidenta Kirgizskoi Respubliki: O dopolnitel'nich merach po sozdaniyu neobchodimych uslovii dlia fuktsionirovaniia gosudarstvennogo i ofitsial'nogo iazkov Kirgizskoi Respubliki" [Decree of the President of the Kyrgyz Republic: On additional measures to create the necessary conditions for the functioning of the state and official languagesof the Kyrgyz Republic]

Akaev's speech at the diplomatic academy of Moscow (15/09/2004a) "Rossiiane mogut ne bezpokoits'sia za sud'bu svoich sootechestvennikov v Kirgizstane" [The Russians don't have to worry about the fate of their compatriots]

Pozharski, V. (15/09/2004b) "Universitet imeni El'tsina" [A university named after Yeltsin]

Akaev's speech at Harvard University (07/10/2004) "Tak teplo o Rossii v garvarde eshcho ne govorili" [In Harvard, no one has spoken yet in such a warm way of Russia]

Akaev's interview to the "Deutsche Welle" (24/11/2004) "Prezident Kirgizstana dal interv'iu 'nemeckoi volne'" [The president of Kyrgyzstan gave an interview to the German wave (Deutsche Welle)]

Nochevki, V. (30/03/2005) "S Putinnym ja uzhe govoril" [I have already talked to Putin]

Interview with the Ambassador of the Russian Federation to the Kyrgyz Republic, E. Shmagin (08/06/2005) "Den' Rossii" [Day of Russia]

V. Bachnyan (14/12/2005): "Razvivaite russkii iazik, eto vam pomozhet ustoiat," [Develop the Russian language – it will you to withstand]

Dosalieva, A. (28/12/2005) "V Moskve budet pamiatnik geroiu eposa Manas" [A monument will be dedicated to the hero of the Manas Epic in Moscow]

Pozhidaev, V. (22/06/2006) "Moskva – Kirgizstan: ot gumanitarnogo sotrudnichestvo k ekonomicheskoi" [Moscow – Kyrgyzstan: from humanitarian cooperation to economic cooperation]

2. Slovo Kyrgyzstana (abb. SK)

Est. 1925 in Frunze (Bishkek), daily newspaper, Russian language;
Former official new organ of the Central Committee of the Communist Party of the Kirgizya;
Chief editor: Alexander Malevany
Circulation: app. 15,000 in 1994, 6000 in 2012;
Affiliation: government

Ashirbaeva, A. (25/07/1992) "Bilet v odin konec" [One way ticket]

Batyrbekov, G. (14/06/1994) "Chemodannoe nastroenie" [travel fever]

Akaev's speech at the KRSU (20/06/1996) "Kyrgyzstan mezhdu velikimi…" [Kyrgyzstan in between great (powers) …]

Akaev's speech at the Congress on "the importance of the Russian language for the community of CIS" (05/03/2004) "Nerushimost sviazei s Velokoi Rossii" [The inviolability oft he strong connection with Great Russia]

Independence Day 2004 - Timeline of Independence 2004 (01/09/2004) "Stanovlenie god za godom – nezavisimomu Kyrgyzstanu – 13 let" [The formation year by year – independent Kyrgyzstan turned 13 years old]

Dosalieva, S. (01/03/2005) "S pravitel'stvom i narodom" [With government and people]

Ashcheulov, D. (05/04/2005) "Krepiat druzhbu internacionalisty," [Internationalists strengthen the friendship]

Turkmenov, U. (10/06/2005) "Manas Kyrgyzstanu pomozhet" [Manas is going to help Kyrgyzstan]

Pavlovich, L. (21/06/2005) "'Ruka Moskvi' v Bishkekskich Shkolach" [Russia's hand in Bishkek's school(s)]

Turkmenov, U. (16/08/2005) "Inauguracionnaia rech Bakieva" [Bakiev's speech at his inauguration ceremony]

Ibraimov, T. (19/08/2005) "Bakiev: Kak dognat i peregnat' samyx sebja [Bakiev: How to catch up with and surpass ourselves]

Mambetov, K. (05/09/2005) "Novii impuls" [New Impulse]

Mambetov, K. (08/09/2005) "Rossiia – Strategicheskii partner" [Russia – Strategic Partner]

Zheenbaev, V., Ploskov, A., Zhunushaldieva, Zh. (24/01/2006) "O kontseptsii novoi gosudarstvennoi ideologii" [On the concept of a new state ideology]

Saidov, A. (23/02/2006) "Na partiinoe pole prishlo "Sodruzhestvo" ["Sodruzhestvo" entered the party landscape]

Party Program of Sodruzhestvo (06/04/2006) "'Sodruzhestvo' – Partiia dostoinogo nastoiashego" ["Sodruzhestvo" – The Party of a Virtuous Present]

Bakiev's official visit to Moscow (25/04/2006) "K. Bakiev: V lice Kyrgyzstana Rossiia imeet nadezhnogo drugo i vernogo soiuznika" [K. Bakiev: In Kyrgyzstan Russia has a reliable friend and truthful ally]

Bolzhurova, È. (28/04/2006) "Sovmestnoe zaiavlenie prezidenta Kyrgyzskoi Respubliki i Prezidenta Rossiiskoi Federatsii" [Joint declaration of the president of the Kyrgyz Republic and the president of the Russian Federation]

Bakiev's address to the parliament (29/09/2006) "Natsional'naia ideologiia est' – nuzhno tol'ko soglasie" [We have a national ideology – all we still need is concordance]

Aychiev, G. (13/06/2007) "Kyrgyzstan – Rossiia: strategicheskie partnery" [Kyrgyzstan – Russia: strategic partners]

Bakiev after joint SCO exercise (18/08/2008) "Kyrgyzstan – Rossiia: Nereshennych problem net" [Kyrgyzstan – Russia: no unresolved problems]

Chinara, S. (26/02/2010) "Prolog suverennogo Kyrgyzstana," [Prologue of a sovereign Kyrgyzstan]

Vlasov, V. (09/02/2010) "Sviazy Rossii s Kyrgyzstanom imeiut sil'nye korni," [The relationship between Russia and Kyrgyzstan has strong roots]

Michailina, G. (10/06/2010) "Vmeste s Rossiei" [Together with Russia]

Shepelenko, A. (06/07/2010) "Sdelaem shag k novoi epoche" [Let's make a step towards a new era]

Asanova, C. (03/09/2010) "Otunbaeva: Mir i soglasie – garant gosudarstvennosti" [Otunbaeva: peace and concord – the guarantee of statehood]

Semenyak, O. (24/09/2010) "Prazdnikom bol'she" [More holidays]

Semenyak, O. (29/09/2010) "Novie prazdniki" [New holidays]

Ansanova, C. (30/12/2010) "Atambaev: 'My tsenim dobruiu voliu Rossii'" [We cherish the benevolence of Russia]

Zhaldukov, G. (28/01/2011) "Mezhnatsional'noe soglasie – bogatstvo strany" [International/Inter-ethnic accord – riches of our country]

Isanov, A. (21/01/2011) "Dve zhizni Kurmanzhan Datki" [The two lives of Kurmanzhan Datka]

Korkmazova, O. (22/02/2011) "Kurmanzhan Datka: gordost' i volnoliubivost'" [Kurmanzhan Datka: Pride and a love of freedom]

Moldalieva, A. (25/02/2011) "Zakon ob epose" [The law on the Epic]

Atambaev's speech at the anniversary of the Great Patriot War (23/06/2011) "Nashe budushchee trebuet edinoi pamiati" [Our future demands a common memory]

Atambaev's speech at Osh State University (21/02/2012) "Almazbek Atambaev: 'Na puti razvitiia Kyrgyzstana stoiat tri osnovnye pregrady – korruptsiia, natsionalizm i mankurtizm'" [On its path of development Kyrgyzstan is facing three major obstacles: corruption, nationalism and mankurtism]

3. Vechernii Bishkek (abb. VB)

Est. 1974 in Frunze (Bishkek), daily newspaper, Russian and Kyrgyz language;
Chief editor: Gennadiy Kuz'min
Circulation: app. 51,000 (38,000 + 13,500) daily
Affiliation: independent

Alianchikov, A. (06/10/1992) "Povroz druzhnee?" [Divided in a more amicable way?]

Yarkov, A. & Denisenkov, E. (22/04/1997) "Vstretimsia u Pushkina" [Let's meet at Pushkin's]

Neshkumai, V. (22/04/1997) "Zdes' pachnet rus'iu" [The spirit of the ancient "rus" is in the air]

Namatbaeva, T. (25/02/1999) "'Popast' v perekrest'e: vnimaniia planety" [Caught in the crosshairs: the attention of the planet]

Yarkov, A. & Denisenkov, E. (08/06/1999) "Pamiatnik vozdvignut rukotvornii" [The monument was erected with bare hands]

Sviridova, S. (10/09/1999) "'Slaviane' v kosmose" [The Slavs out in space]

Turdubaev, T. (25/05/2000) "Bez iazyka – na chemodanach" [Without language – on (their) suitcases]

Turdubaev, T. (25/05/2000) "V obshchem dome – choziiaev net" [There are no lords in the common home]

4. Kyrgyz-Tuusu (abb. K-T)

Est. 1924 in Frunze (Bishkek), daily newspaper, Kyrgyz language;
Chief editor: Abdikamit Matisakov
Circulation: app. 16,000 in 2012;
Affiliation: government

(08/05/2000) "Sabïrduu Ak Sanatay Sayasat," [Discrete and wise policy]

List of Interviewees

Interviews were conducted between July 20 and September 14, 2014, in Bishkek, Kyrgyz Republic.

	Name	Occupation/Position
1.	Ms. Ainura Bekkoenova	Dimension Chief, Democratic Governance Program UNDP Kyrgyzstan.
2.	Professor Abylabek Asankanov	Head of Department of Anthropology at Kyrgyz National University and Co-author of the 2013 "Concept of National Unity and Inter-ethnic relations." He has written extensively on Kyrgyz ethno-genesis and national identity.
3.	*Anonymous*	Senior member of "Ar-Namyz" Party (Chairman: Felix Kulov, Prime Minister under President Bakiev 2005–2007) *14,2 %, 25 seats in Zhogorku Kenesh (2014).*
4.	Ms. Asel' Kalybekova	Freelancer, i.a. at Eurasianet.org.
5.	Dr. Elmira Nogoibaeva	Analyst at Research Center „Polis" Asia.
6.	*Anonymous*	Representative of the State Department for Inter-Ethnic Relations of the Kyrgyz Republic, founded during the Interim-Presidency of Rosa Otunbaeva.
7.	Mr. Murataly Uchkempirov	Chief of Dimension "Cooperation with Youth Organizations" at the Ministry of Labor, Migration and Youth of the Kyrgyz Republic.
8.	Professor Andrew Wachtel	President of the American University of Central Asia. He has contributed considerably to the studies of nationalism and cultural politics in the Balkans, and also written on minority issues in Kyrgyzstan.

	Name	Occupation/Position
9.	Ms. Perizat Suranova	Deputy Director of the Political Council of the Zamandash Party. Founded in 2007, Zamandash claims to represent the interests of Kyrgyz labor migrants working in Russia and Kazakhstan. Zamandash is explicitly inclusive – some of its leading members are ethnic Russians – and favorable towards Russia, where so many of its voters work (cf. Diatlenko 2012).
10.	Ms. Asel' Doolotkeldieva	Research Associate at the National Institute for Strategic Studies of the Kyrgyz Republic (NISI), Assistant to NISI Director Talant Sultanov, PhD candidate at University of Exeter.
11.	Mr. Shukhrat Aytiev	Former personal assistant to Kamchybek Tashiev, presidential candidate in 2011 as head of Ata-Zhurt party. Currently, Aytiev is member of the Ata-Zhurt fraction in the Kyrgyz parliament (Zhogorku Kenesh).
12.	*Anonymous*	Former Advisor to the Head of Presidential Administration of the Kyrgyz Republic.
13.	Mr. Ravshan Zheenbekov	Non-affiliated Member of Parliament (Zhogorku Kenesh). 1998–99, he held the position of Deputy Chairman of the State Committee of Foreign Investments. In 2001, he became Deputy Chief of Staff of Akaev's presidential administration. After the Tulip Revolution in 2005, he represented the Kyrgyz Republic as ambassador to Malaysia for two years. From 2010 to 2013, acted as Deputy Chairman of the "Ata-Meken" fraction in parliament.
14.	Mr. Nurbek Toktakunov	Director of the Kyrgyz Law firm "Precedent," Web Activist and Blogger.
15.	Dr. Marat Kazakhbaev	Political Scientist, Lecturer at Russian-Slavonic University, Kyrgyz National University.
16.	Mr. Olivier Ferrando	Research Fellow at Sciences Po Paris.

	Name	Occupation/Position
17.	Mr. Edil Baisalov	Chief of Staff to the 3rd president and head of the interim government in Kyrgyzstan, Roza Otunbaeva, following the 2010 Kyrgyzstani uprising on April 7, 2010. He is a Kyrgyz political activist and former president of the Coalition for Civil Society and Democracy, a leading civic advocacy group that publicly criticized the growing links between the Akaev administration and organized crime networks in Kyrgyzstan.
18.	Anonymous	Former Press Secretary of the Kyrgyz Government.
19.	Ms. Asel Murzakulova	Lecturer at Bishkek Humanitarian University, Publications on nationalism and civic education.
20.	Ms. Dina Maslova	Head Editor of "Vechernij Bishkek" online edition (vb.kg).
21.	Anonymous	Representative of the Kyrgyz "Association of Young Entrepreneurs".
22.	Professor Tyntchtybek Chorotegin	Kyrgyz historian, publicist and journalist. From 2003 to 2010, he was the director of the Kyrgyz service of Radio Free Europe/Radio Liberty (Radio Azattyk). From 2012–2013, he was the president of the Kyrgyz history society, and is currently an independent researcher.
23.	Anonymous	Senior member of the Cultural Center of Uzbeks in Kyrgyzstan.
24.	Anonymous	Former advisor to the OSCE High Commissioner on National Minorities.
25.	Mr. Ryskeldi Satke	Freelancer, blogger and contributing writer with research institutions and news organizations in Central Asia, Turkey and the U.S.
26.	Anonymous	---
27.	Mr. Aleksandr Ivanov	Head of the Russian Unifying Union of Compatriots (*Glava Russkogo ob'edinitel'nogo soiuza sootechestvennikov*).
28.	Mr. Giorgio Fiacconi	Honorary Consul of Italy to the Kyrgyz Republic, Businessman, Founder and Editor in Chief of the Times of Central Asia.

www.ingramcontent.com/pod-product-compliance
Lightning Source LLC
Chambersburg PA
CBHW051102230426
43667CB00013B/2413